# THE USBORNE
# DOT-TO-DOT
# BOOK

Karen Bryant - Mole and Jenny Tyler
Illustrated By Graham Round

# DOT-TO-DOT
## ON THE
# FARM

# Arriving at the farm

Cat and mouse are visiting frog's farm.

- Join the blue, green, orange and red dots to find out how they got there.
- Join the yellow dots to find the farmhouse.
- Who is running to meet them?
  Join the brown dots to find out.

1 2 3 4 5 6 7 8 9 10 11 12 13 14 15 16 17 18 19 20 21 22 23 24 25

# The pigsty

Cat and mouse are visiting the pigs.

- Join the pink, brown and yellow dots to find them.
- Who is sharing the pigs' dinner? Join the red dots to find out.

1 2 3 4 5 6 7 8 9 10 11 12 13 14 15 16 17 18 19 20 21 22 23 24 25

- Join the green dots to find out what mouse is doing.

- Cat is bringing the pigs a surprise. What is it?

- Can you find something odd in the pigsty? Join the blue dots and see what it is.

# A surprise visit

- Who are cat and mouse visiting now? Join the red, green and yellow dots to find out.

- Join the blue dots to help you see what cat is doing.

- Who is hiding in the hen house? Join the dots to see.

# Lunch time

- Cat and mouse are having lunch at the farm.
- Join the red dots to find out who is sitting at the table with them.

1 2 3 4 5 6 7 8 9 10 11 12 13 14 15 16 17 18 19 20 21 22 23 24 25

- Join the pink, blue and yellow dots to find out what there is to eat.

- Who is hiding under the table? Join the green dots to find out.

26 27 28 29 30 31 32 33 34 35 36 37 38 39 40 41 42 43 44 45 46 47 48 49 50

# A walk in the field

After lunch, cat goes for a walk across the field.

- Join the blue dots to see what he has taken with him.
- Join the red dots to find out who he sees on the way.

1 2 3 4 5 6 7 8 9 10 11 12 13 14 15 16 17 18 19 20 21 22 23 24 25

- Join the green dots to see who is hiding in the tree.
- Who is eating the seeds? Join the orange dots to find out.
- Join the brown dots to see who is looking over the hedge.

# At the pond

- Join the dots to answer these questions:
- Who is hiding in the reeds?
- What is flying across the pond?
- What has cat caught?
- What is mouse doing?
- Who is jumping out of the water?

1 2 3 4 5 6 7 8 9 10 11 12 13 14 15 16 17 18 19 20 21 22 23 24 25

# In the orchard

- What is elephant pushing?
  Join the red and brown dots to find out.

- Join the blue dots to make something for
  mouse to stand on.

- What can you see when you join the green dots?

- Join the yellow dots to make something to put the apples
  in and the orange dots for something for cat to stand on.

1 2 3 4 5 6 7 8 9 10 11 12 13 14 15 16 17 18 19 20 21 22 23 24 25

# Frog's problem

- Join the green dots to find out what frog is driving. What has happened to it?

- Cat is coming to help. Join the yellow dots to see what he is carrying.

1 2 3 4 5 6 7 8 9 10 11 12 13 14 15 16 17 18 19 20 21 22 23 24 25

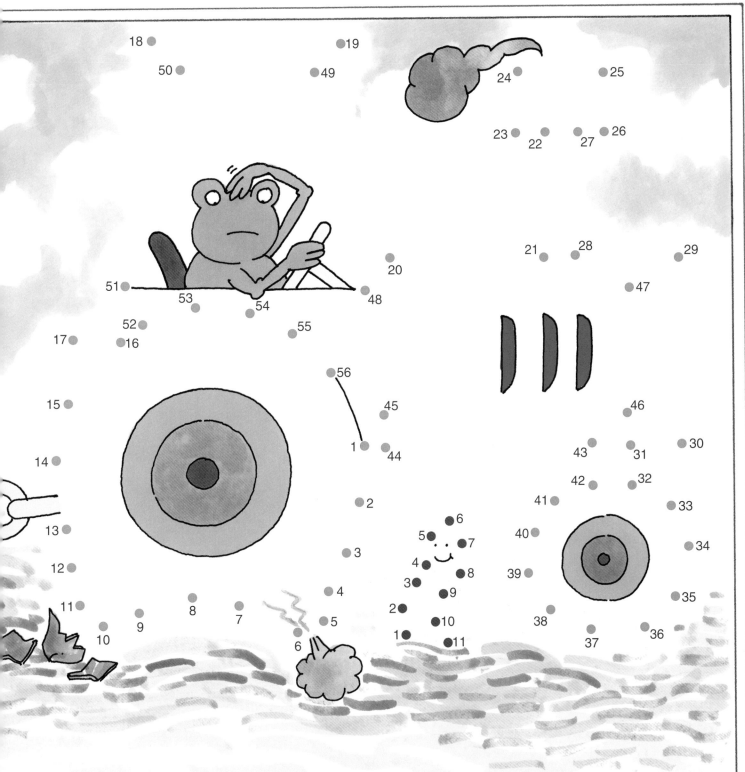

- Join the orange and pink dots to find out what the tractor is pulling and who is in it.

- Who is hiding under the tractor? Join the dots to find out.

# In the sheep field

- Join the dots and see how many sheep you can find.
- Someone is chasing the sheep. Who is it?

1 2 3 4 5 6 7 8 9 10 11 12 13 14 15 16 17 18 19 20 21 22 23 24 25

● Can you see who is hiding among the sheep?

# Harvest time

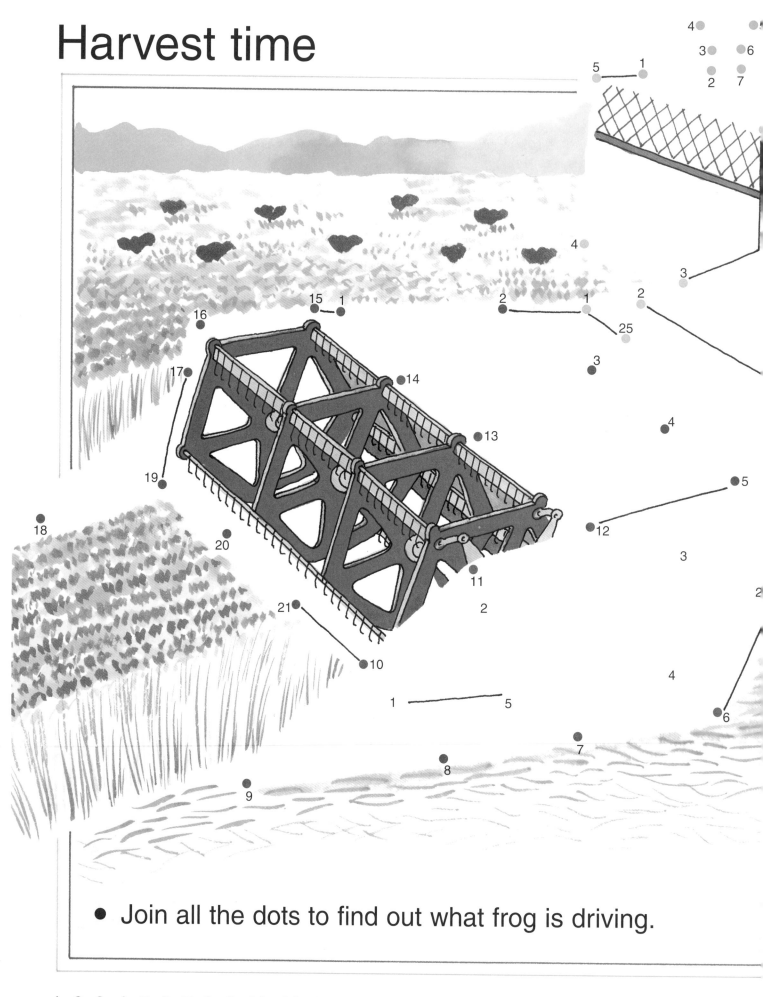

• Join all the dots to find out what frog is driving.

1 2 3 4 5 6 7 8 9 10 11 12 13 14 15 16 17 18 19 20 21 22 23 24 25

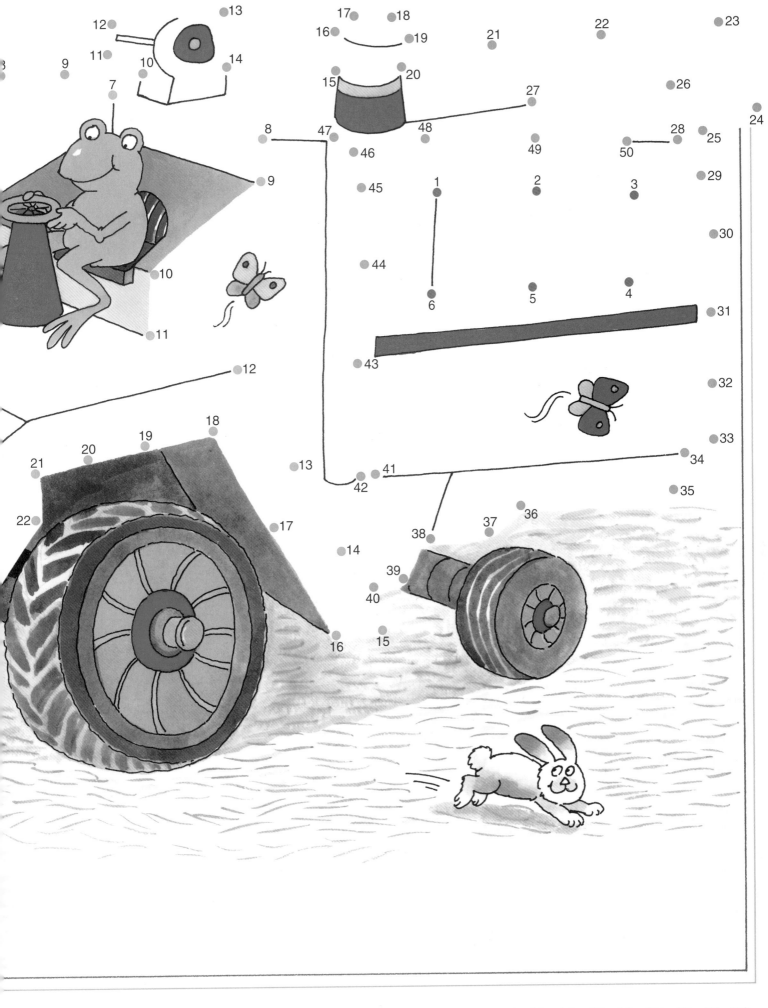

# At the show

Frog's animals have won some prizes at the show.

- Who has won 1st prize?
- Who has won 2nd prize?
- Who has won 3rd prize?

1 2 3 4 5 6 7 8 9 10 11 12 13 14 15 16 17 18 19 20 21 22 23 24 25

- Join the dots to see which vegetable has won 1st prize.

- Which vegetables came 2nd?

- Which vegetable came 3rd?

26 27 28 29 30 31 32 33 34 35 36 37 38 39 40 41 42 43 44 45 46 47 48 49 50

# Going home

Cat and mouse are waving goodbye to the animals.

● Join the dots to find out how they are going to get home.

# DOT-TO-DOT
## ON THE
# SEASHORE

# On the way

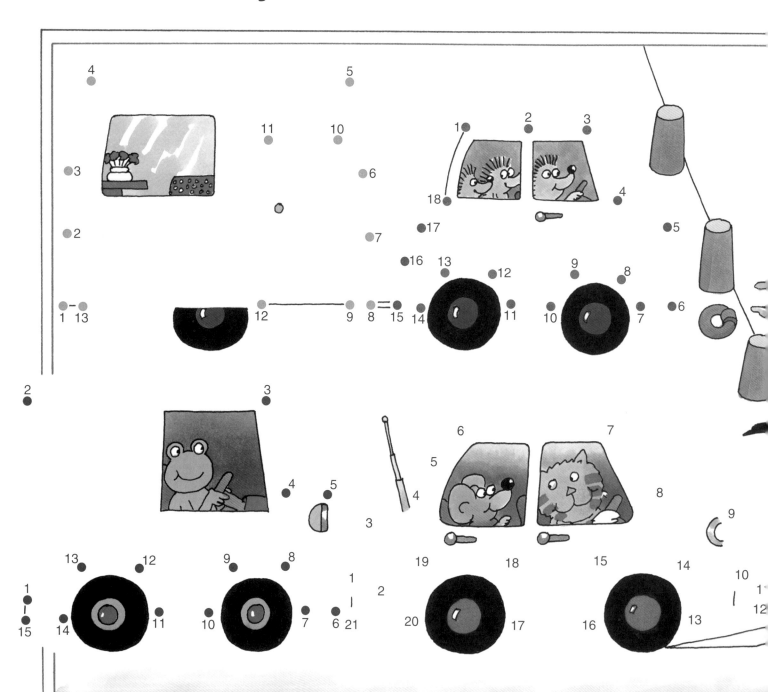

Cat and mouse are going to spend a week at the seaside. On the way they have to go on a car ferry.

- Join the blue dots to see what the ferry looks like.
- Join the yellow dots to see cat's car.
- What is frog driving? Join the purple dots to find out.

1 2 3 4 5 6 7 8 9 10 11 12 13 14 15 16 17 18 19 20 21 22 23 24 25 26

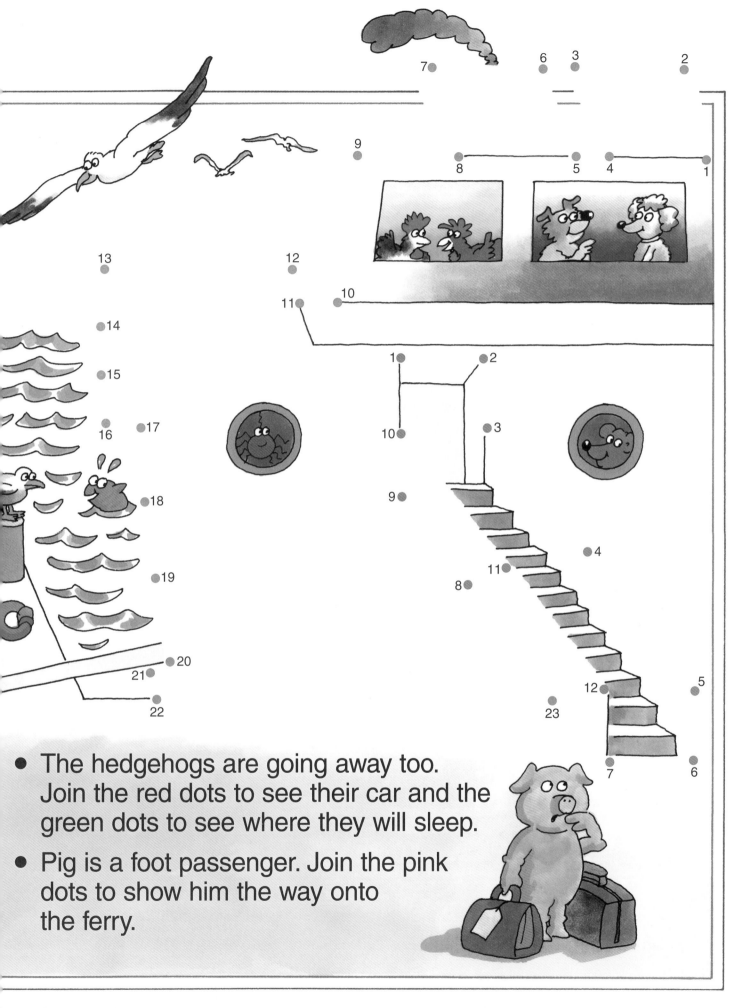

- The hedgehogs are going away too. Join the red dots to see their car and the green dots to see where they will sleep.

- Pig is a foot passenger. Join the pink dots to show him the way onto the ferry.

27 28 29 30 31 32 33 34 35 36 37 38 39 40 41 42 43 44 45 46 47 48 49 50

# The house by the sea

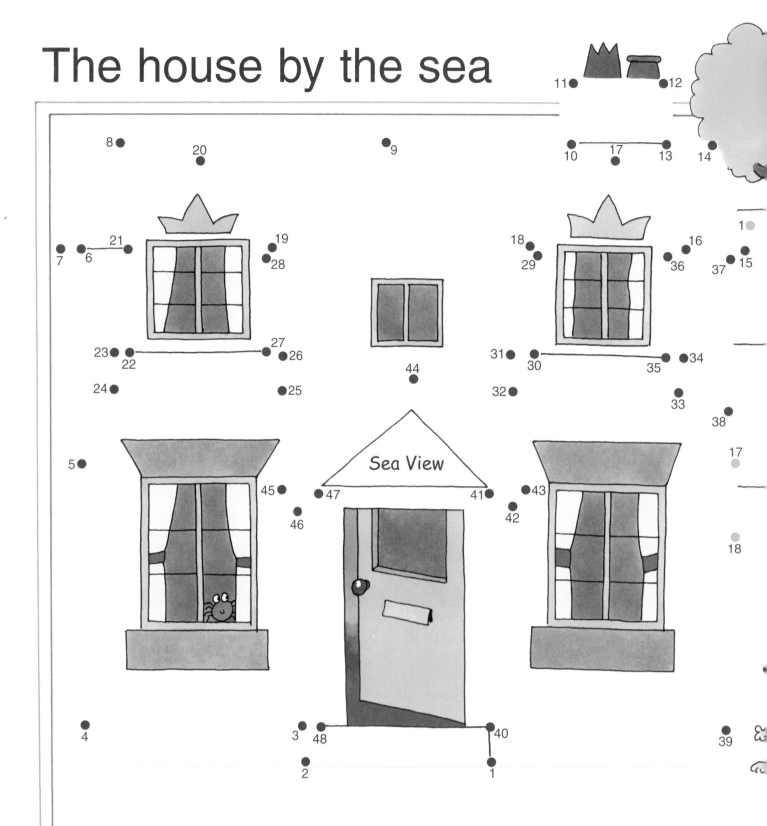

Cat and mouse have rented a house for the week.

- Join the brown dots to see what it looks like.
- Can you see what the house is called?

1 2 3 4 5 6 7 8 9 10 11 12 13 14 15 16 17 18 19 20 21 22 23 24 25 26

- The house has a terrace overlooking the bay. Find it by joining the green dots.

- What can you see if you join the yellow dots?

27 28 29 30 31 32 33 34 35 36 37 38 39 40 41 42 43 44 45 46 47 48 49 50

# On the beach

- Mouse has been busy. Join the yellow dots to see what he has been doing.
- Join the red and blue dots to see what he used.
- Cat and mouse have had a picnic. Join the green dots to find their picnic hamper.
- Join the orange dots to find someone who would like to help finish the picnic.

1 2 3 4 5 6 7 8 9 10 11 12 13 14 15 16 17 18 19 20 21 22 23 24 25 26

# In the water

- What is cat doing? Join the yellow dots to find out.
- Join the green dots to find out what the hedgehogs are doing.
- Who is splashing? Join the blue dots to see.

1 2 3 4 5 6 7 8 9 10 11 12 13 14 15 16 17 18 19 20 21 22 23 24 25 26

- Join the red dots to see what is lying on the beach.
- Who has fallen out of his boat?

27 28 29 30 31 32 33 34 35 36 37 38 39 40 41 42 43 44 45 46 47 48 49 50

# A rock pool

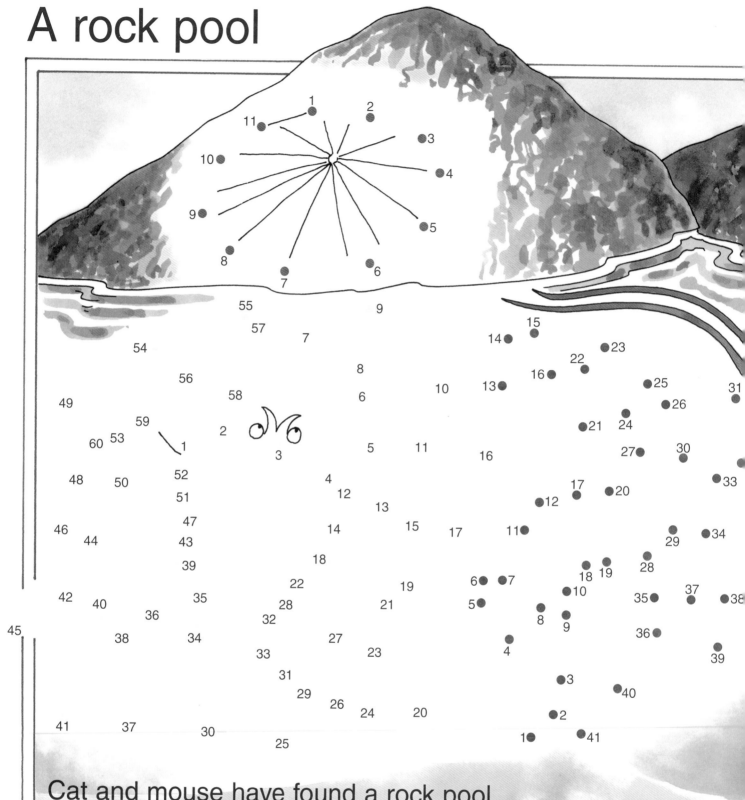

Cat and mouse have found a rock pool.

- Join the yellow dots to find something that lives there.
- Join the green dots to see a shrimp.
- Join the red dots to see a sea plant.

1 2 3 4 5 6 7 8 9 10 11 12 13 14 15 16 17 18 19 20 21 22 23 24 25 26

- If you join the blue dots you will see an animal that looks like a plant. It is called a sea anenome.

- Limpets stick very tightly to rocks. You can see one by joining the pink dots.

# Watersports

8
9
10
11
12
7
6
3
13
5
32  14
4
4
3
30  31
28  29
26  27
2
24  25
2
22  23
20  21
5
1
19
18
17
16

6
7  1  8  9
11  10
22

21
20
13
19  12
18
14

15
17  16

- Join the red and green dots to see what mouse is doing.
- What is cat doing? Join the yellow dots to see.
- Join the blue and purple dots to see what the other animals are doing.

1 2 3 4 5 6 7 8 9 10 11 12 13 14 15 16 17 18 19 20 21 22 23 24 25 26

# The beach café

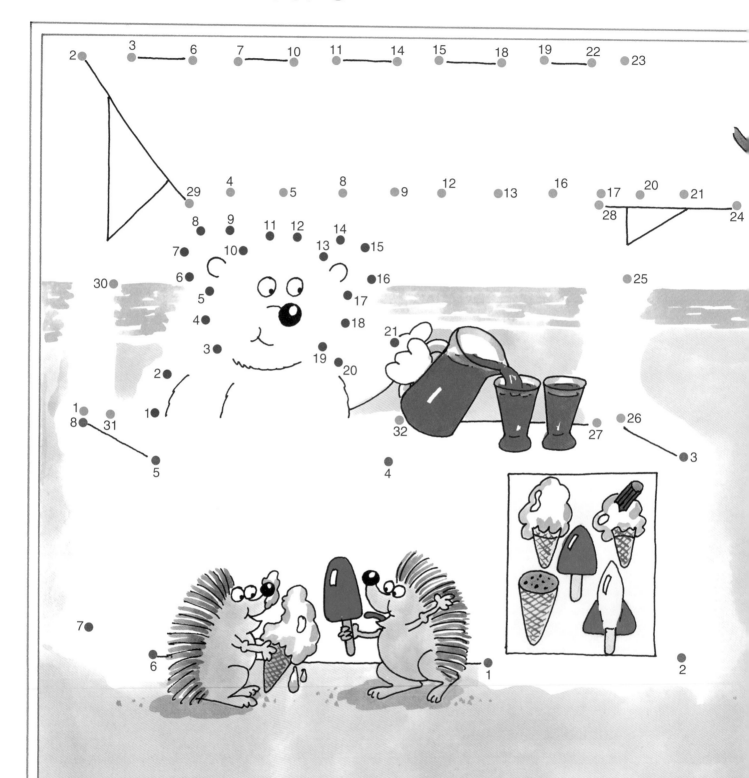

- Join the green and red dots to see the beach café.
- Who is pouring out drinks? Join the brown dots to see.
- Join the yellow dots to see what mouse has ordered.

1 2 3 4 5 6 7 8 9 10 11 12 13 14 15 16 17 18 19 20 21 22 23 24 25 26

- Join the blue dots to shade cat and mouse from the sun.
- Finish drawing their table by joining the orange dots.
- Mouse has lost his sunglasses. Can you find them?

27 28 29 30 31 32 33 34 35 36 37 38 39 40 41 42 43 44 45 46 47 48 49 50

# The port

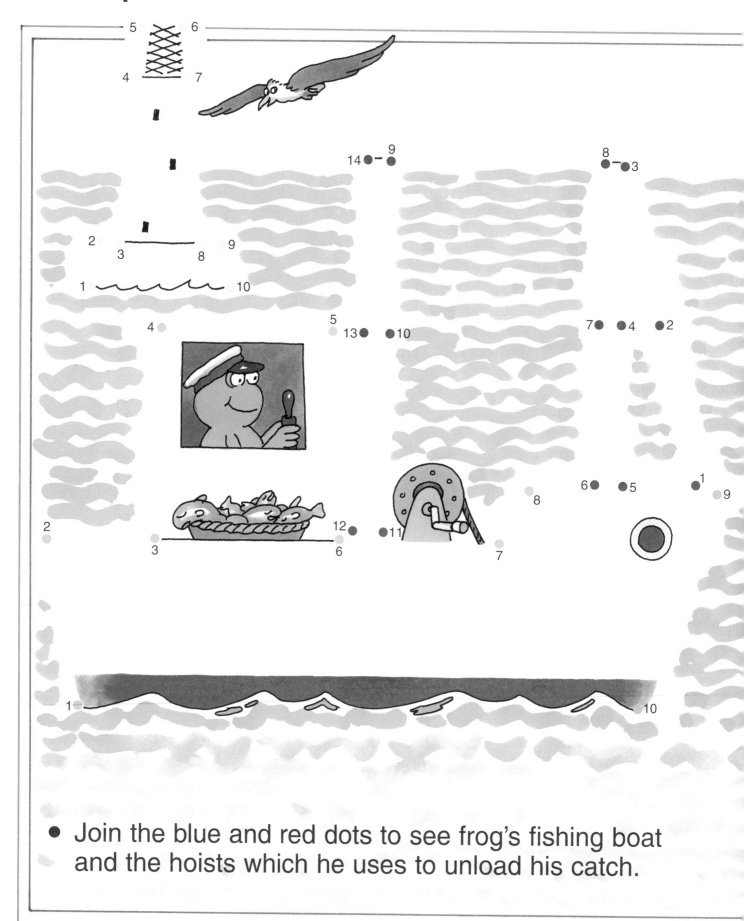

- Join the blue and red dots to see frog's fishing boat and the hoists which he uses to unload his catch.

1 2 3 4 5 6 7 8 9 10 11 12 13 14 15 16 17 18 19 20 21 22 23 24 25 26

- Join the pink dots to find something which floats on air.
- What can you see if you join the yellow dots?

# Underwater

Cat and mouse are scuba diving.

● Join the yellow dots to find out what cat is looking at.

9    10                    20

8              11              19              21

7              12

5              13

6              18

70            14    17

22

15    16

62            23

69            28

54            36

63            44

53            35

61            45              29

37

55    52    46              34    27

56            43    38    30    25

51    47              33    31    26

39

50    48    42

40    32

49

41

5

4              6

3

2              7    8

1              9

17              12    11

16              13

15

14

10

● Join the blue and green dots to see an eel and a
   flat fish.

● What has mouse found? Join the purple dots to see.

27  28  29  30  31  32  33  34  35  36  37  38  39  40  41  42  43  44  45  46  47  48  49  50

# On the cliffs

Cat and mouse are going for a cliff walk.

- Join the blue dots to see who mouse is photographing.
- What can you see if you join the yellow dots?

1 2 3 4 5 6 7 8 9 10 11 12 13 14 15 16 17 18 19 20 21 22 23 24 25 26

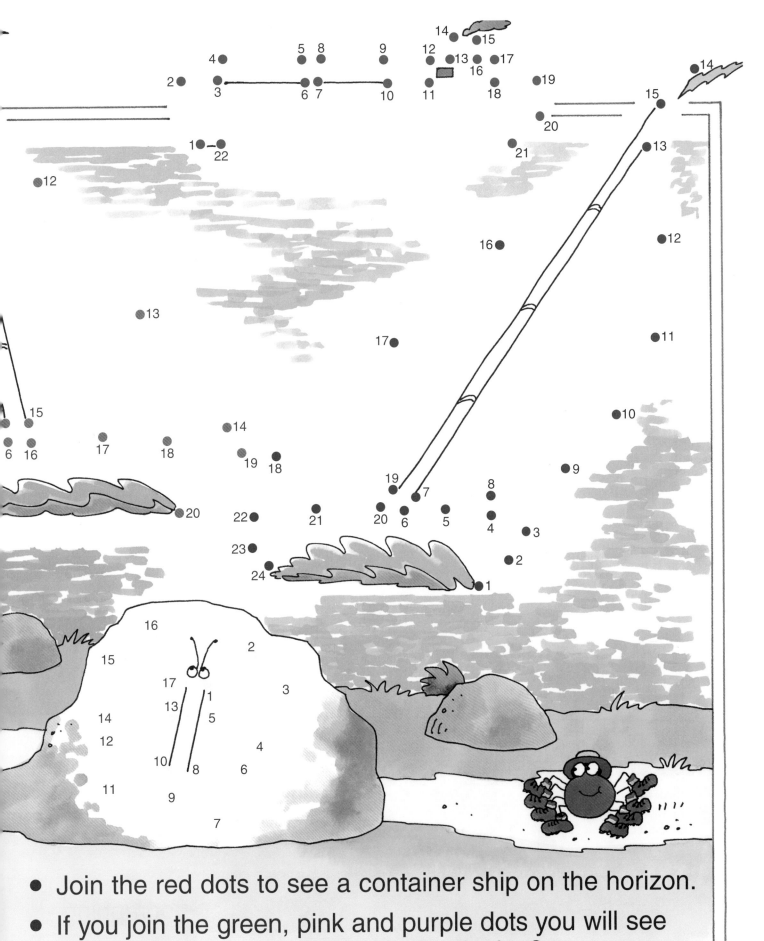

- Join the red dots to see a container ship on the horizon.
- If you join the green, pink and purple dots you will see some yachts racing. Which one is winning?

# Buying souvenirs

Beach Bazaar

Cat and mouse are looking for presents to take home.

● What can you see if you join the dots?

1 2 3 4 5 6 7 8 9 10 11 12 13 14 15 16 17 18 19 20 21 22 23 24 25 26

# The Shell Shack

- Join the green and orange dots to see some gifts that are decorated with shells.

- Join the pink and yellow dots to finish the Shell Shack.

# Home again

Cat and mouse are unpacking.

- Join the blue and yellow dots to see their suitcases.
- Join the green dots to see what cat bought himself at the Beach Bazaar.
- What did mouse buy at the Shell Shack? Join the red dots.

# DOT-TO-DOT
# ANIMALS

# Cat and mouse set off

1 2 3 4 5 6 7 8 9 10 11 12 13 14 15 16 17 18 19 20 21 22 23 24 25 26

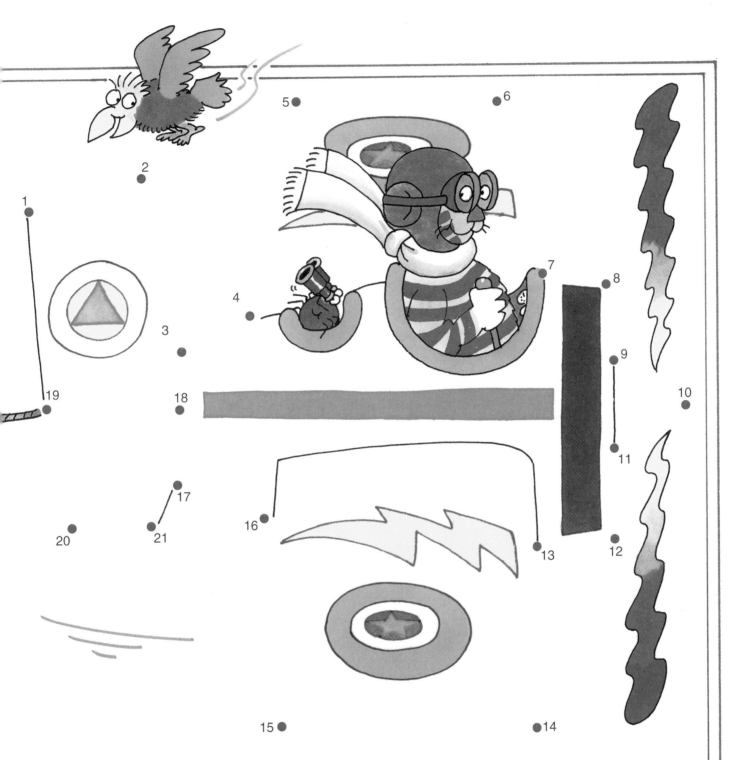

Cat and mouse are going on an expedition to see how many different animals they can find.

- Join the red and blue dots to find out how they are travelling.

- Join the yellow dots to see what spider is doing.

28 29 30 31 32 33 34 35 36 37 38 39 40 41 42 43 44 45 46 47 48 49 50

# In the rainforest

Cat and mouse have landed in the hot, steamy rainforest.

- Join the red dots to find a rainforest bird.

- Do you know what the largest kind of ape is called?
  Join the blue dots to find one.

1 2 3 4 5 6 7 8 9 10 11 12 13 14 15 16 17 18 19 20 21 22 23 24 25 26

- Join the green dots to find out which animal is hiding in the grass.

- Join the yellow dots to find another animal. What is it?

- Can you find another animal with stripes?

# In the garden

Cat and mouse have flown in to help with the gardening.

- Join the blue dots to see an animal which started life as a caterpillar.

1 2 3 4 5 6 7 8 9 10 11 12 13 14 15 16 17 18 19 20 21 22 23 24 25 26

- Join the yellow, green and brown dots.

- Which animal has eight feet? Which animal has no feet? Which animal has one foot?

# Underwater adventure

Cat and mouse are exploring underwater in a submarine.

- Join the red dots to see what it looks like.
- Which undersea animal has eight legs?
  Join the yellow dots to find out.

1 2 3 4 5 6 7 8 9 10 11 12 13 14 15 16 17 18 19 20 21 22 23 24 25 26

- Join the blue dots to find a dolphin.
- Find two more undersea animals by joining the green and orange dots. What are they?

# On safari

Cat and mouse are on safari in the grasslands of Africa.

- Join the green and red dots to see what they are travelling in.

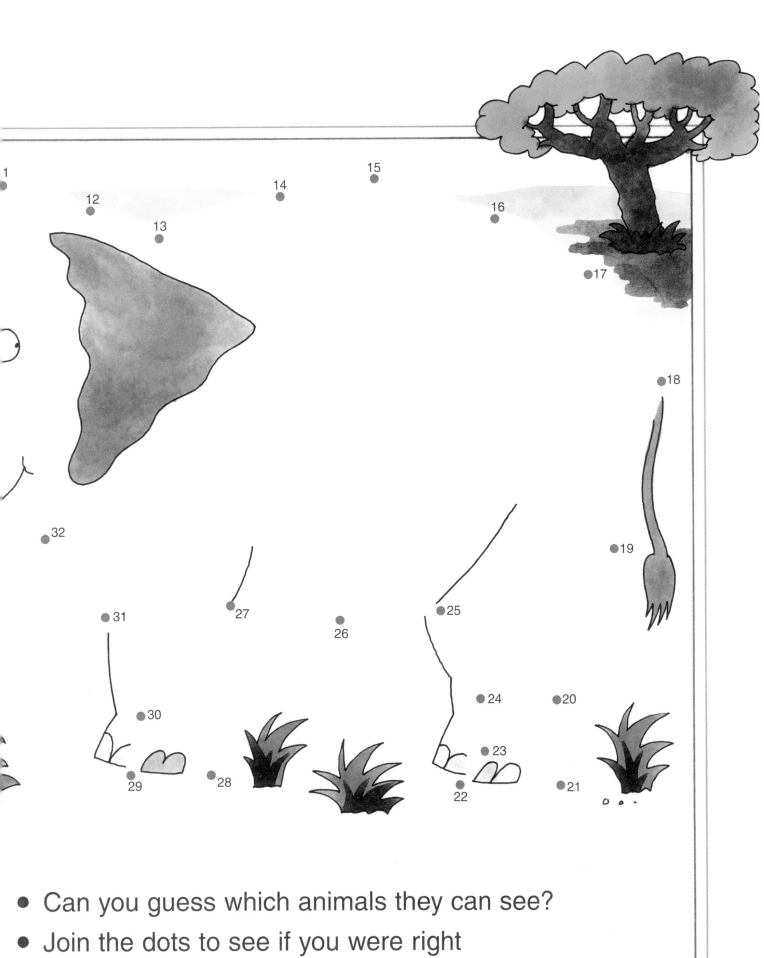

- Can you guess which animals they can see?
- Join the dots to see if you were right

28 29 30 31 32 33 34 35 36 37 38 39 40 41 42 43 44 45 46 47 48 49 50

# At the seaside

- Cat has been busy.
  Join the yellow dots to find out what he has been doing.

- Join the pink dots to discover why mouse has dropped his ice cream.

1 2 3 4 5 6 7 8 9 10 11 12 13 14 15 16 17 18 19 20 21 22 23 24 25 26

- Where is frog? Join the red dots to find out.
- What can you see if you join the blue dots?
- Join the orange dots to find out what is lying on the beach.

28 29 30 31 32 33 34 35 36 37 38 39 40 41 42 43 44 45 46 47 48 49 50

# Under the ground

Cat and mouse are investigating life under the ground.

- Mouse has found an animal whose home is called a set.

- Join the blue dots to find out what it is.

- Join the green dots to find its set.

1 2 3 4 5 6 7 8 9 10 11 12 13 14 15 16 17 18 19 20 21 22 23 24 25 26

- Which animal lives in a den? Join the brown dots to find out.
- Join the orange dots to see its den.
- There are two more animals to find.
  Join the dots to see what they are.

# By the river

- Join the orange dots to find an otter.
- Otters live in river banks.
  Join the green dots to see the edge of this river bank.
- Join the yellow dots. What can you see?

1 2 3 4 5 6 7 8 9 10 11 12 13 14 15 16 17 18 19 20 21 22 23 24 25 26

- Do you know what a kingfisher looks like? Join the blue dots to find out.

- When you join the red dots you will find something with two sets of wings. Do you know what it is called?

# At the farm

Cat and mouse are visiting a farm.

- What is cat doing? Join the blue dots to help you to see.
- Who is hiding inside the henhouse?

1 2 3 4 5 6 7 8 9 10 11 12 13 14 15 16 17 18 19 20 21 22 23 24 25 26

- What is mouse doing? Join the brown dots to find out.
- Join the others dots to find some more farm animals.

# An icy expedition

Cat and mouse have arrived in the frozen North.

- Join the red dots to see how they got there.

- Join the blue dots to see where they will stay.

- Who is cat playing snowballs with? Join the yellow dots to se

1 2 3 4 5 6 7 8 9 10 11 12 13 14 15 16 17 18 19 20 21 22 23 24 25 26

- What is mouse doing?
  Join the green dots to find out.

- Join the orange and brown dots to find two more
  animals that live in cold places. What are they?

# In the forest

Cat and mouse are walking through the forest.

- Join the red dots to see something they must not touch.
- Join the pink and green dots to find two woodland birds.
- Join the blue dots to see spider's home.

1 2 3 4 5 6 7 8 9 10 11 12 13 14 15 16 17 18 19 20 21 22 23 24 25 26

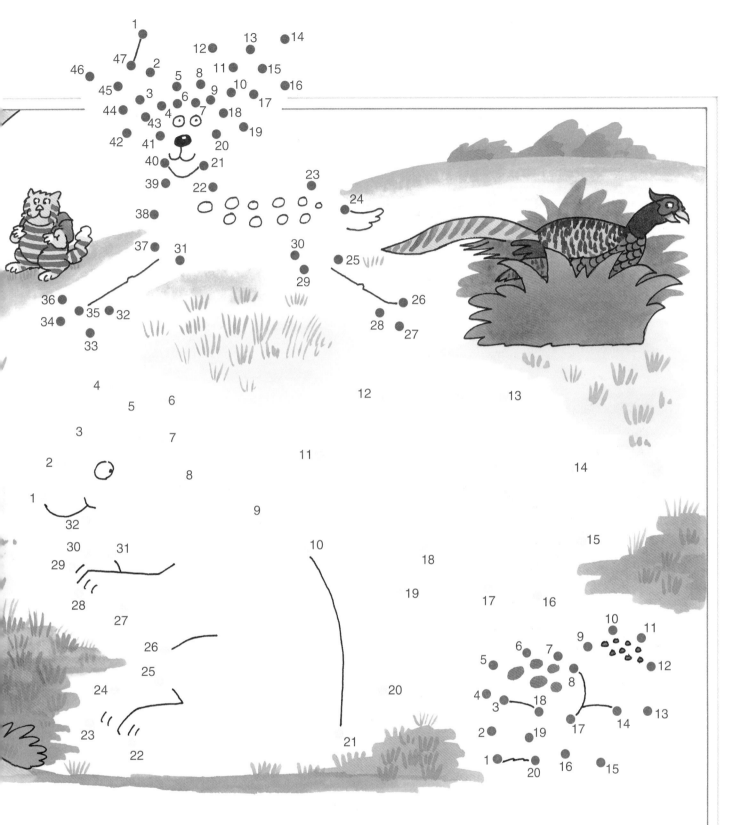

- Which animal lives in trees and eats nuts?
  Join the yellow dots to find out.

- Join the brown dots to see an animal whose babies
  are called fawns.

# Home again

Cat and mouse are coming home after their exciting expedition.

- What is mouse pushing? Join the dots to see.
- Can you see how many suitcases they have brought with them?

# DOT-TO-DOT
# DINOSAURS

# First life

Life on our planet began in the sea.

- Join the blue dots to see one of the first animals. It is called a trilobite.

- Join the orange dots to see an animal which you can still find in the sea today.

1 2 3 4 5 6 7 8 9 10 11 12 13 14 15 16 17 18 19 20 21 22 23 24 25

- A sponge is an animal that looks like a plant.
  Join the purple dots to find one.

- Join the red dots to see a prehistoric fish.

- You can see a sea scorpion by joining the yellow dots.

26 27 28 29 30 31 32 33 34 35 36 37 38 39 40 41 42 43 44 45 46 47 48 49 50

# Life comes ashore

Some of the first land animals were fish which developed lungs and strong fins to pull themselves along the ground.

- Join the green dots to see a lung fish called Eusthenopteron.
- Join the blue dots to see Ichthyostega, which was an amphibian. Amphibians can live both on land and in water.

51 52 53 54 55 56 57 58 59 60 61 62 63 64 65 66 67 68 69 70 71 72 73 74 75

There were lots of giant insects around at this time too.

- Join the red dots to see a cockroach, the yellow dots to see a spider and the purple dots to see a huge dragonfly.

- Can you find cat and mouse?

# The first reptiles

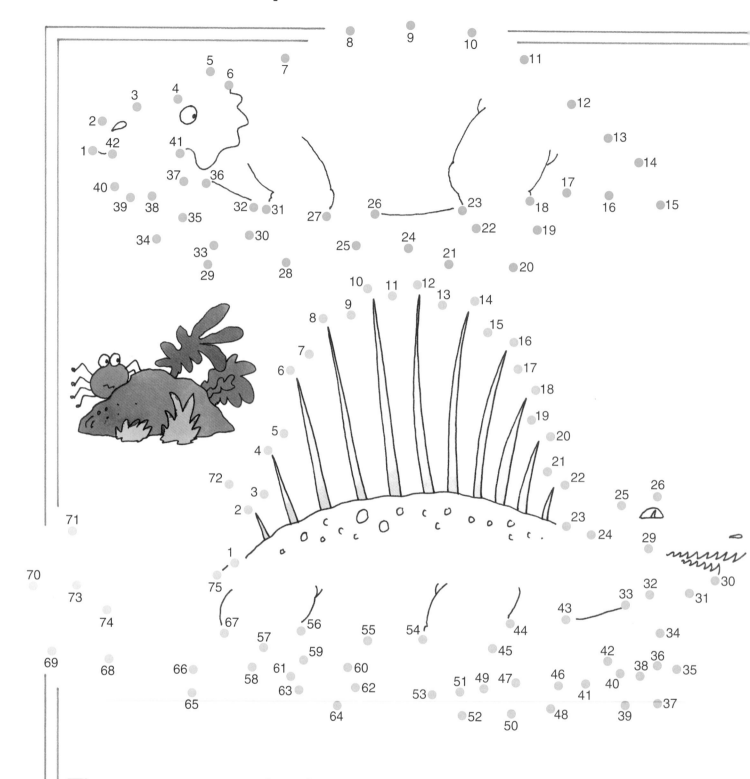

The next group of animals to appear were the reptiles.
Reptiles have dry, scaly skins and lay eggs with shells.

- Join the green dots to find Pareiasaurus. This was one of the first plant-eating reptiles.

1 2 3 4 5 6 7 8 9 10 11 12 13 14 15 16 17 18 19 20 21 22 23 24 25

- Join the yellow dots to see an Araeoscelis.

Some of the reptiles had large sails on their backs. These probably helped them to warm up by soaking up the sun's rays.

- Join the blue dots to see Dimetrodon, which ate meat. Join the red dots to see Edaphosaurus, which ate plants.

26 27 28 29 30 31 32 33 34 35 36 37 38 39 40 41 42 43 44 45 46 47 48 49 50

# Early dinosaurs

These dinosaurs all lived in the age called the Triassic period.

- Join the blue dots to see a tiny dinosaur called Saltopus.
- If you join the green dots you will see a big Plateosaurus.

51 52 53 54 55 56 57 58 59 60 61 62 63 64 65 66 67 68 69 70 71 72 73 74 75

- Coelophysis was slim with a long neck and tail. Join the yellow dots to see what it looked like.

- The dinosaur you see when you join the red dots is called Anchisaurus.

# The giants

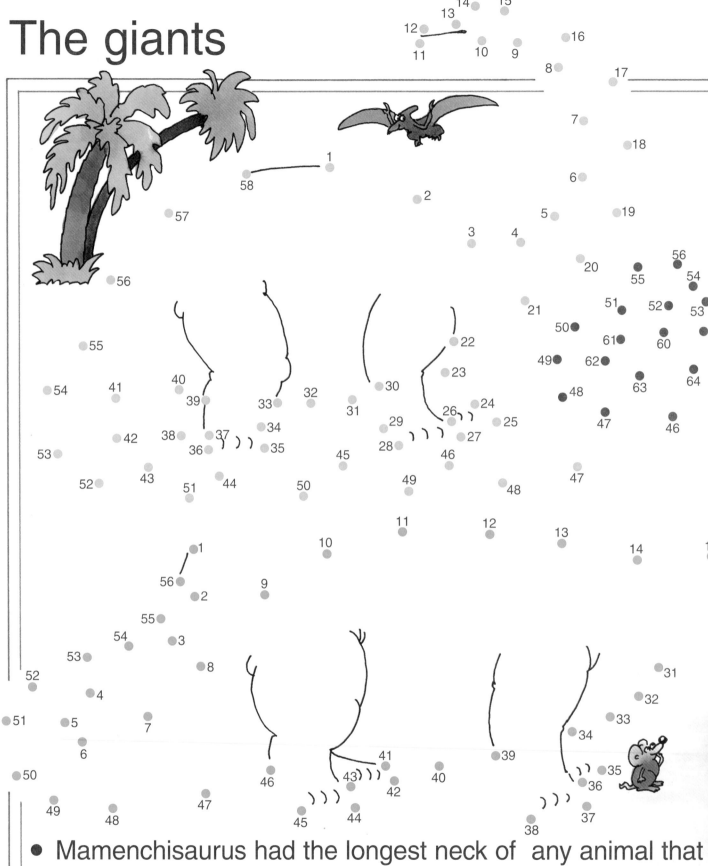

- Mamenchisaurus had the longest neck of any animal that has ever lived. Join the green dots to see this dinosaur.

- Join the red dots to find the tallest dinosaur, Brachiosaurus.

1  2  3  4  5  6  7  8  9  10  11  12  13  14  15  16  17  18  19  20  21  22  23  24  25

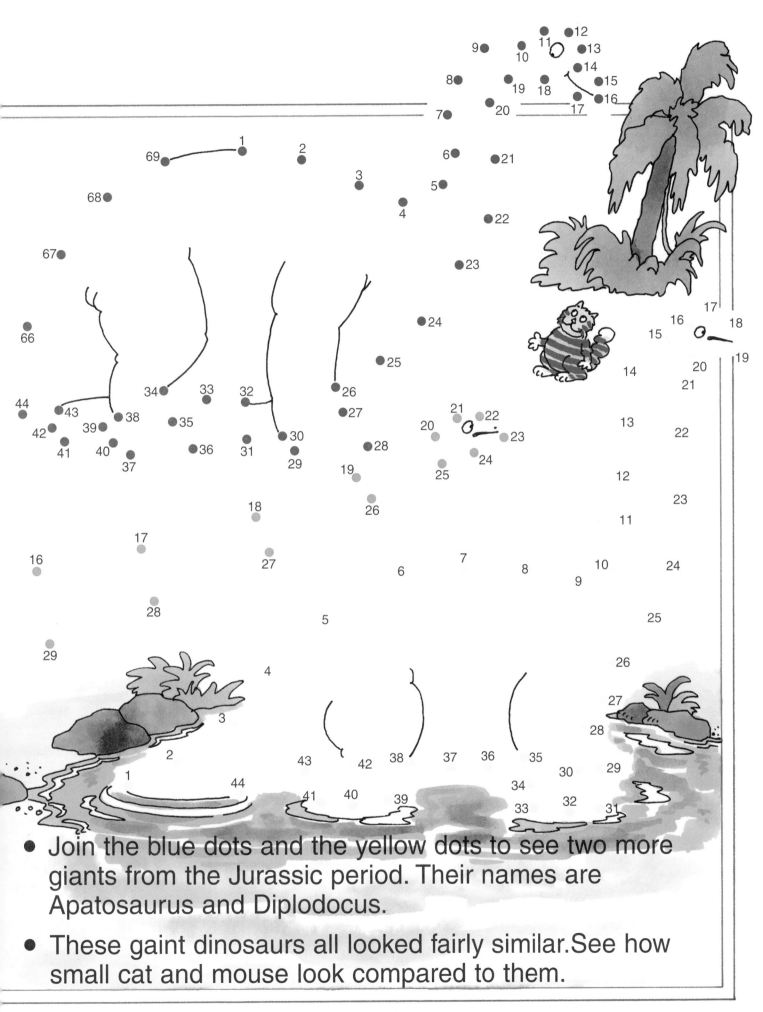

- Join the blue dots and the yellow dots to see two more giants from the Jurassic period. Their names are Apatosaurus and Diplodocus.

- These gaint dinosaurs all looked fairly similar. See how small cat and mouse look compared to them.

26 27 28 29 30 31 32 33 34 35 36 37 38 39 40 41 42 43 44 45 46 47 48 49 50

# By the water

- Cat has spotted Allosaurus, one of the main meat-eating Jurassic dinosaurs. Join the red dots to see it.

- Join the green dots to see Compsognathus which was only the size of a hen.

51 52 53 54 55 56 57 58 59 60 61 62 63 64 65 66 67 68 69 70 71 72 73 74 75

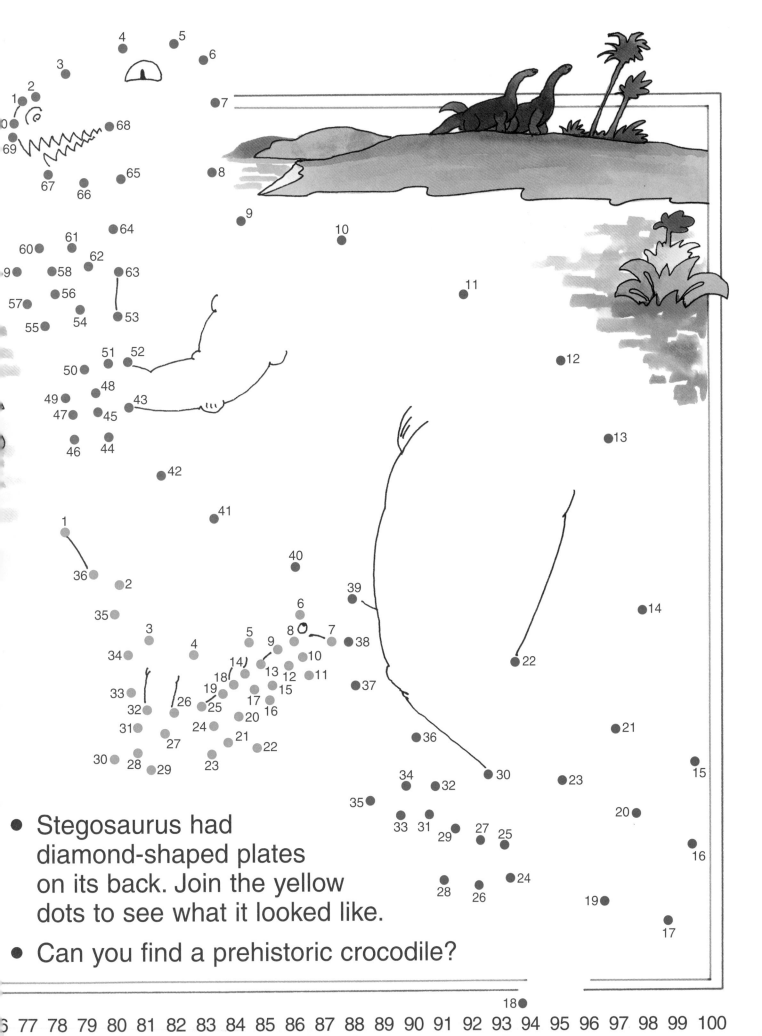

- Stegosaurus had diamond-shaped plates on its back. Join the yellow dots to see what it looked like.

- Can you find a prehistoric crocodile?

# In the air

Flying reptiles are called pterosaurs.

- Join the green dots to see the pterosaur Dimorphodon.
- Join the orange dots to find another pterosaur called Rhamphorhynchus.

1 2 3 4 5 6 7 8 9 10 11 12 13 14 15 16 17 18 19 20 21 22 23 24 25

- Pterodactylus was a small pterosaur. It was about the size of a starling. Join the red dots to see one.

- If you join the blue dots you will see Archaeopteryx. Many people say that it was the first real bird.

# Sea monsters

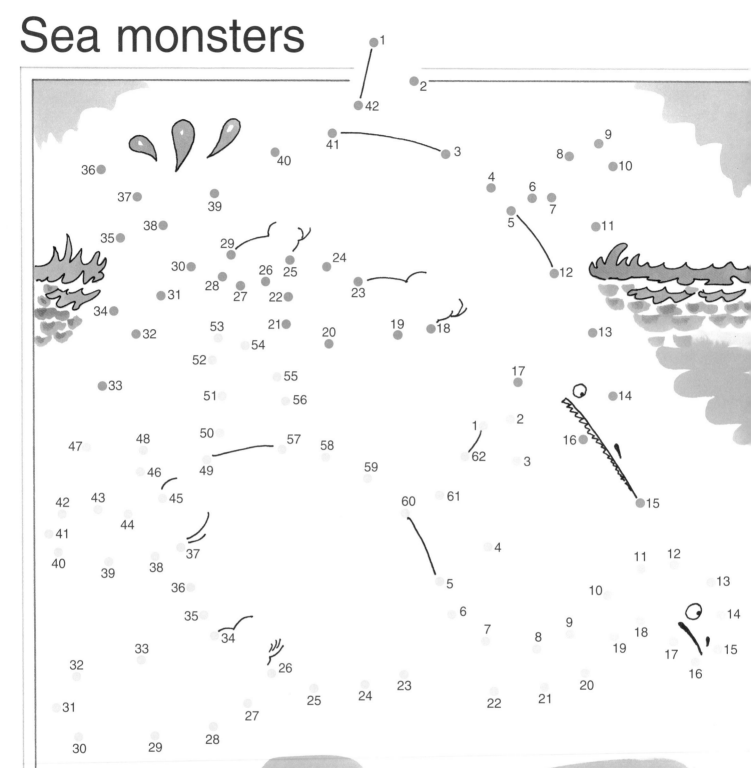

Plesiosaurs and pliosaurs were sea reptiles which lived at the same time as dinosaurs.

- Join the yellow dots to find a long-necked plesiosaur called Cryptoclidus.

- Join the blue dots to see a pliosaur called Liopleurodon.

51 52 53 54 55 56 57 58 59 60 61 62 63 64 65 66 67 68 69 70 71 72 73 74 75

- If you join the green dots you will find an Ichthyosaurus. Its name means "fish lizard".

- Join the red dots to see the enormous turtle, Archelon.

# Plated dinosaurs

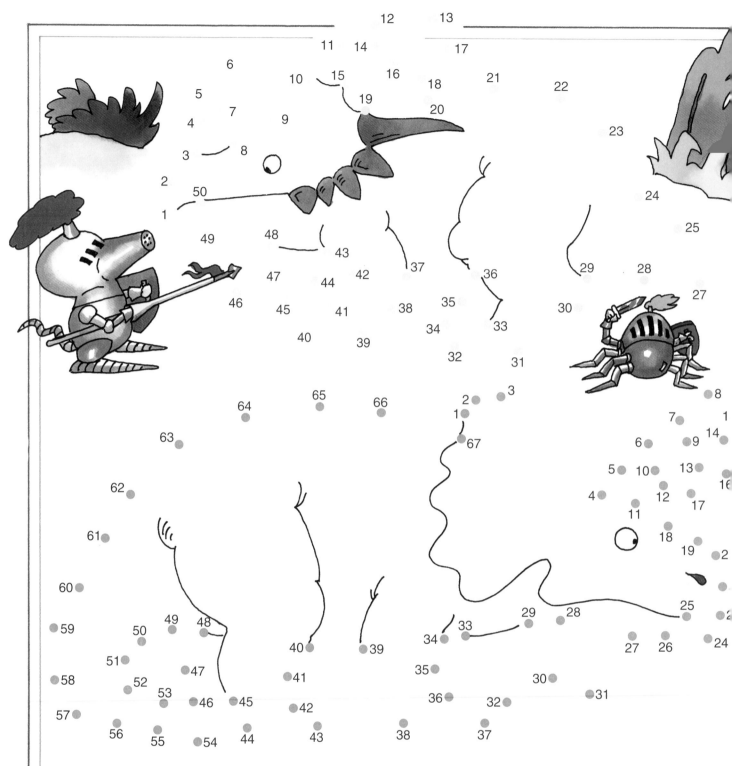

Some of the dinosaurs had protective plates to shield them from other dinosaurs.

- Join the blue dots to see Triceratops and the yellow dots to find Styracosaurus.

1 2 3 4 5 6 7 8 9 10 11 12 13 14 15 16 17 18 19 20 21 22 23 24 25

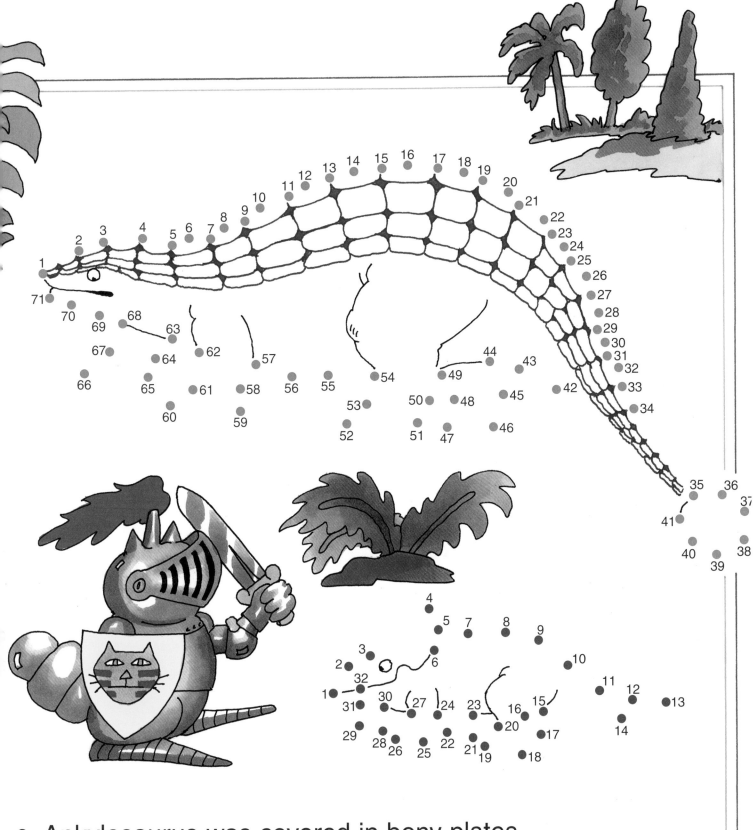

- Ankylosaurus was covered in bony plates.
  It used the large bones on the end of its tail as a club.
  Join the green dots to see one.

- Join the red dots to see a small dinosaur called Protoceratops.

# More large dinosaurs

- Tyrannosaurus was probably the fiercest of all the dinosaurs. Find out what it looked like by joining the yellow dots.

- Parasaurolophus had a long bony crest on its head. Join the green dots to see this strange dinosaur.

51 52 53 54 55 56 57 58 59 60 61 62 63 64 65 66 67 68 69 70 71 72 73 74 75

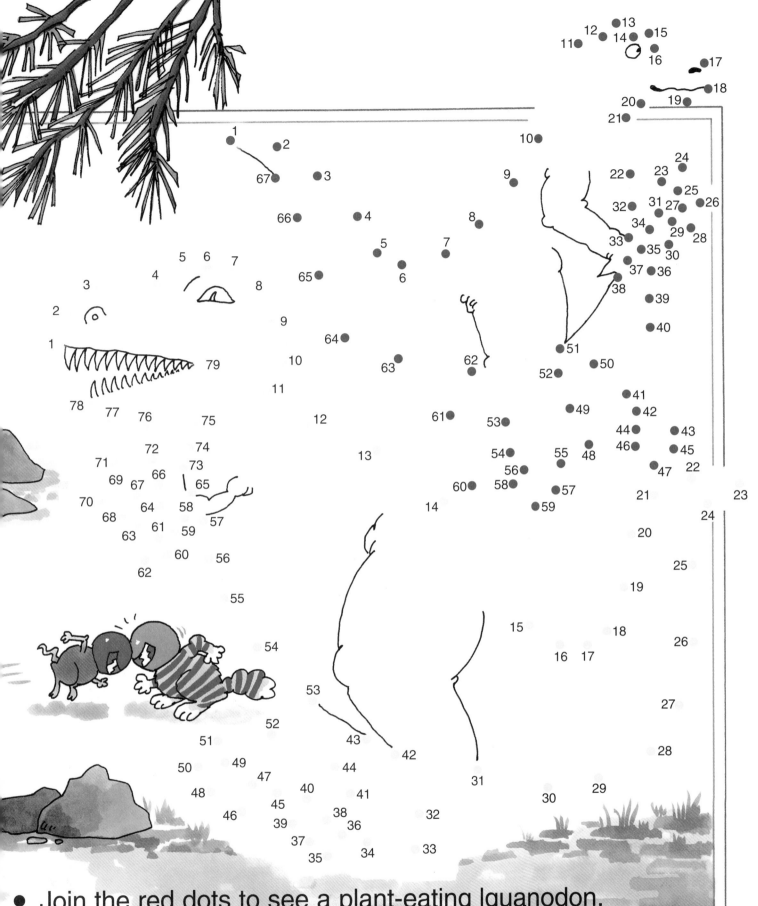

- Join the red dots to see a plant-eating Iguanodon.
- Pachycephalosaurus may have used its thick skull in fights. Join the blue dots to see it.

76 77 78 79 80 81 82 83 84 85 86 87 88 89 90 91 92 93 94 95 96 97 98 99 100

# Some smaller dinosaurs

Here are some dinosaurs that look fairly similar.

- Join the red dots to see the long-tailed Ornithomimus.

- Stenonychosaurus was one of the most intelligent dinosaurs. You can find one by joining the yellow dots.

1 2 3 4 5 6 7 8 9 10 11 12 13 14 15 16 17 18 19 20 21 22 23 24 25

- Join the blue and green dots.
One of these dinosaurs is called Deinonychus and eats
meat with its sharp teeth. The other is a plant-eater with a
bony beak called Hypsilophodon. Which is which?

# Saying the names

Allosaurus
Al-oh-saw-rus

Coelophysis
See-low-fy-sis

Eusthenopteron
Yews-then-op-tur-on

Ornithomimus
Or-nith-oh-my-mus

Saltopus
Salt-oh-puss

Anchisaurus
An-kee-saw-rus

Compsognathus
Komp-sog-nay-thus

Hypsilophodon
Hips-ill-offa-don

Pachycephalosaurus
Pak-ee-sef-al-oh-saw-rus

Stegosaurus
Steg-oh-saw-rus

Ankylosaurus
An-ky-low-saw-rus

Cryptoclidus
Krip-oh-kly-dus

Ichthyostega
Ik-thee-oh-saw-rus

Parasaurolophus
Para-saw-rollo-fuss

Stenonychosaurus
Sten-on-ik-oh-saw-rus

Apatosaurus
A-pat-oh-saw-rus

Deinonychus
Dy-non-ee-kus

Ichthyostega
Ik-thee-oh-stee-ga

Pareiasaurus
Par-eye-a-saw-rus

Styracosaurus
Sty-rack-oh-saw-rus

Araeoscelis
A-ray-oh-sell-iss

Dimetrodon
Dee-mee-tro-don

Plateosaurus
Plat-ee-oh-saw-rus

Triceratops
Try-ser-a-tops

Archaepteryx
Are-kee-op-tur-iks

Dimorphodon
Die-more-foe-don

Iguanodon
Ig-wa-no-don

Protoceratops
Pro-toe-ser-a-tops

Trilobite
Try-low-bite

Archelon
Ar-ke-lon

Diplodocus
Dip-lo-doe-kus

Liopleurodon
Lee-oh-plu-roe-don

Pterodactylus
Ter-oh-dak-til-us

Brachiosaurus
Brack-ee-oh-saw-rus

Edaphosaurus
Eda-foe-saw-rus

Mamenchisaurus
Ma-men-ke-saw-rus

Rhamphorhynchus
Ram-foe-rin-kus

Tyrannosaurus
Tie-ran-oh-saw-rus

# DOT-TO-DOT
# MACHINES

# Factory machines

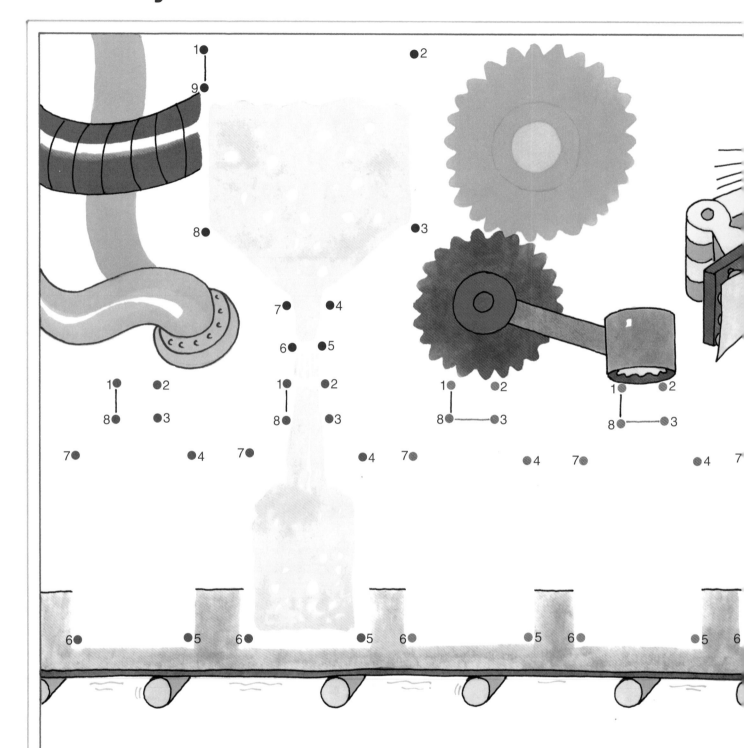

Cat and mouse are working in the lemonade factory.

- Join the red, brown, orange, pink, yellow and blue dots to see the bottles on the conveyor belt.

- What is the machine doing to the bottles?

1 2 3 4 5 6 7 8 9 10 11 12 13 14 15 16 17 18 19 20 21 22 23 24 25

- Join the black dots to see the part of the machine that fills the bottles with lemonade. You can fill in the bottles with a yellow pencil.

- What is mouse doing? Join the green dots to find out.

# Racing machines

1 2 3 4 5 6 7 8 9 10 11 12 13 14 15 16 17 18 19 20 21 22 23 24 25

- Join the red and green dots to find two very fast machines.
- Join the yellow dots to see something that goes slowly.

# Building machines

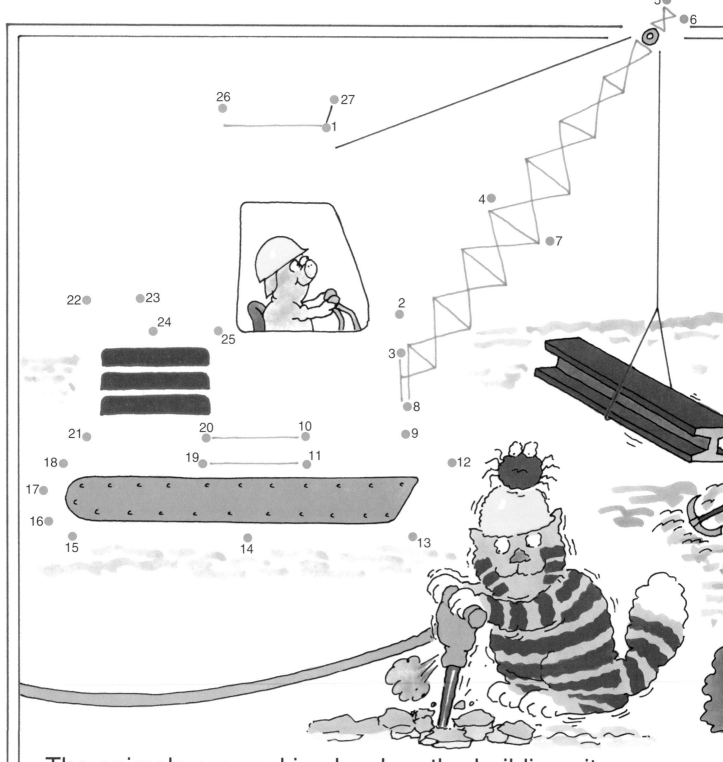

The animals are working hard on the building site.

- Join the green dots to see the machine pig is using to lift a heavy girder. What is this machine called?

- What can you see if you join the blue dots?

1 2 3 4 5 6 7 8 9 10 11 12 13 14 15 16 17 18 19 20 21 22 23 24 25

- What is mouse doing?
  Join the yellow dots to find out.

- Join the red dots.
  Do you know what this machine is called?

# Machines in the air

The animals are going flying.

- Join the yellow dots to find out what cat is flying in.

1 2 3 4 5 6 7 8 9 10 11 12 13 14 15 16 17 18 19 20 21 22 23 24 25

- Join the red dots and green dots. What can you see?
- One of these machines is a plane and the other is a glider. Planes have engines. Gliders have very long wings and no engines. Which is mouse flying?

# Road machines

- What is bear driving? Join the green dots to find out.
- Join the yellow and orange dots to find out what frog is driving.

1 2 3 4 5 6 7 8 9 10 11 12 13 14 15 16 17 18 19 20 21 22 23 24 25

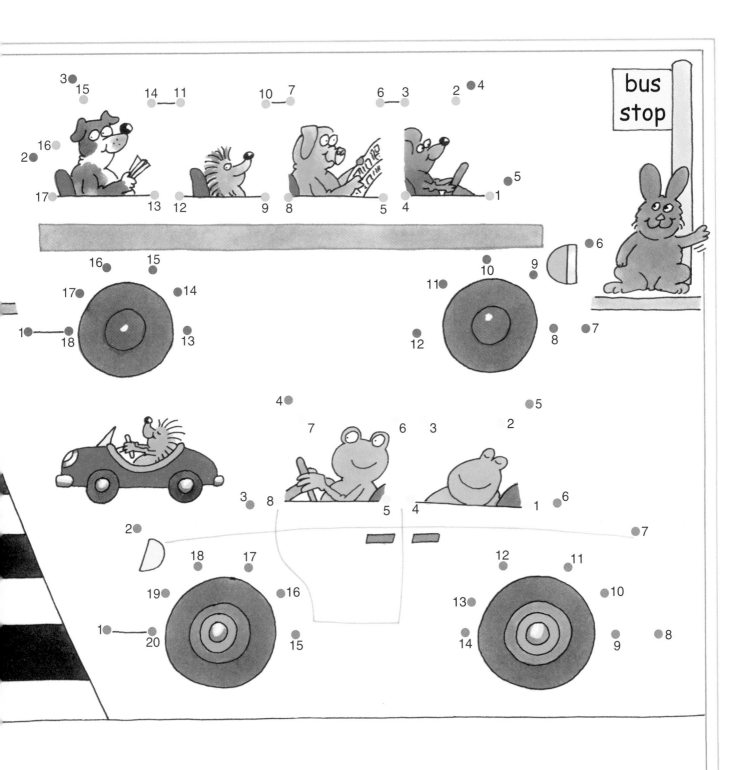

bus
stop

- Join the red dots to see what mouse is driving.
- Join the blue dots to help his passengers see out.

# Machines at sea

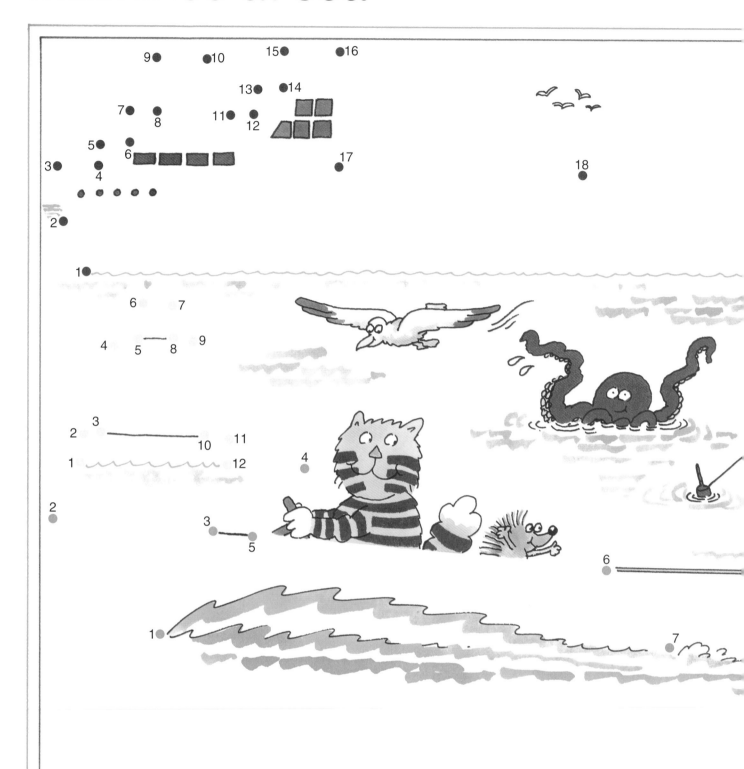

- Can you find an oil tanker, a fishing boat, a speedboat and a passenger ship in this picture?

- Join the red, blue, green and orange dots to see them all.

1 2 3 4 5 6 7 8 9 10 11 12 13 14 15 16 17 18 19 20 21 22 23 24 25

- Join the yellow dots. What can you see?
  (It is a buoy which warns ships of dangerous rocks under the water.)

- Who is water skiing?

# Steam machine

Can you guess what the animals are doing now?

- Cat is driving a steam engine. Join the green dots to see what is looks like.

- The engine has a very hot coal fire in it. This heats water to make steam and the steam makes the engine go.

1 2 3 4 5 6 7 8 9 10 11 12 13 14 15 16 17 18 19 20 21 22 23 24 25

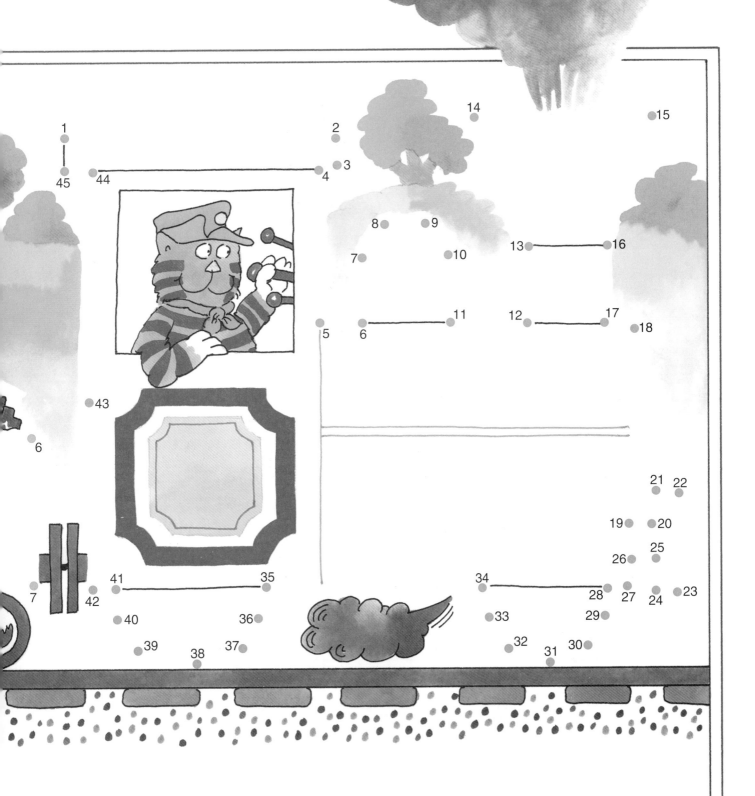

- Join the blue dots to see where the coal is stored. Whose job is it to put the coal on the fire?

- Join the red and yellow dots to find out what the passengers are sitting in.

26 27 28 29 30 31 32 33 34 35 36 37 38 39 40 41 42 43 44 45 46 47 48 49 50

# Space machines

Cat and mouse have landed on a strange planet.

- Join the red dots to see cat's spacesuit.
- Join the green dots and you will see his landing craft.

1 2 3 4 5 6 7 8 9 10 11 12 13 14 15 16 17 18 19 20 21 22 23 24 25

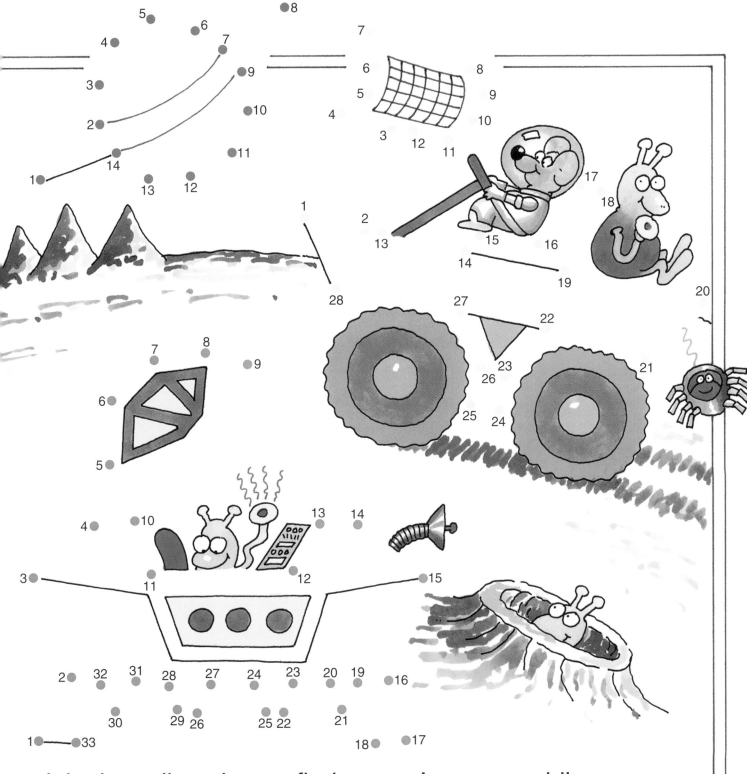

- Join the yellow dots to find mouse's spacemobile. Can you see its radar?

- Where is hedgehog? Join the blue dots to find out.

- What can you see when you join the orange dots?

# Emergency machines

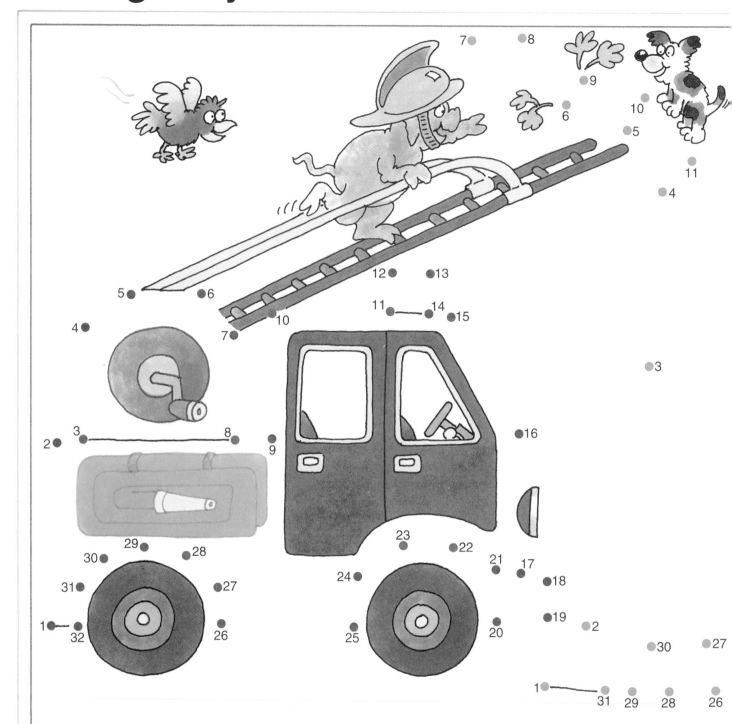

Dog is very worried.

- Join the green dots to see where her puppy is.
- Who is coming to the rescue?

1 2 3 4 5 6 7 8 9 10 11 12 13 14 15 16 17 18 19 20 21 22 23 24 25

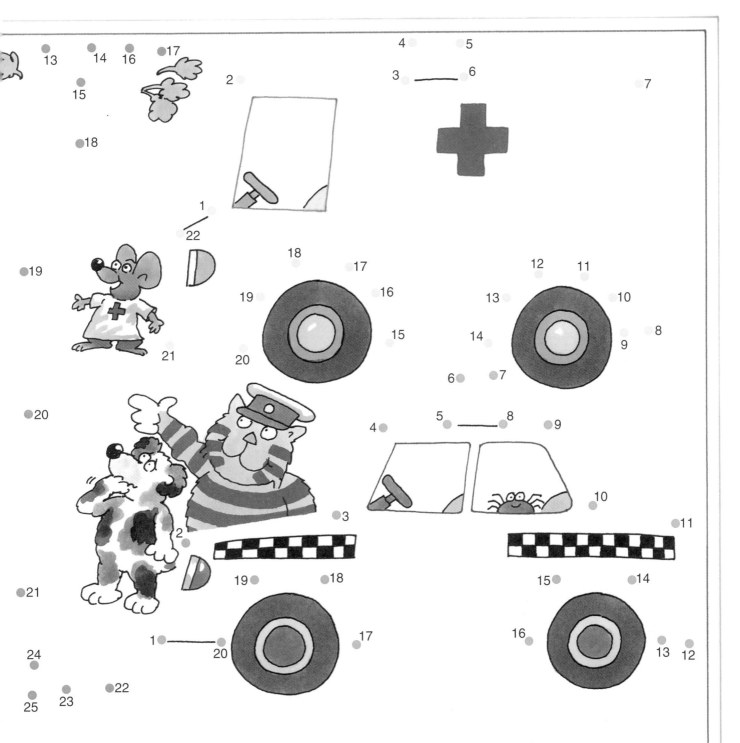

- Join the red dots to find out if you were right.
- Join the yellow and blue dots to see who else has arrived to help.
- Can you spot spider?

# Fairground machines

Cat is buying a ticket to go on the merry-go-round.

- What animals are there to ride on?
  Join the red, blue and yellow dots to find out.

1 2 3 4 5 6 7 8 9 10 11 12 13 14 15 16 17 18 19 20 21 22 23 24 25

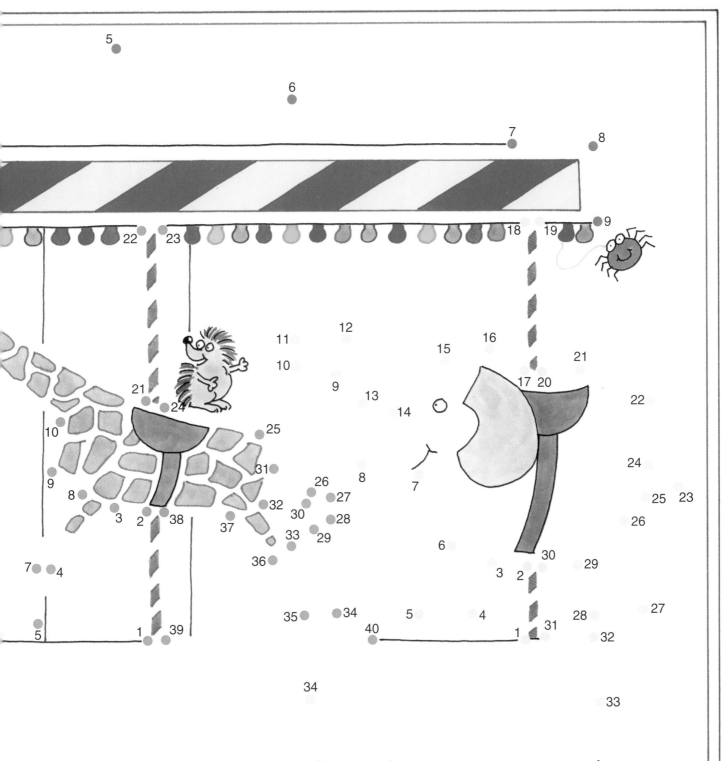

- Join the orange dots to finish the merry-go-round.
- What other fairground machine can you see when you join the green dots?

# Toy machines

The animals are testing toys in the toy shop.

- Cat hasd found a remote-controlled toy. What is it?
  Join the orange dots and both sets of green dots to see.

1 2 3 4 5 6 7 8 9 10 11 12 13 14 15 16 17 18 19 20 21 22 23 24 25

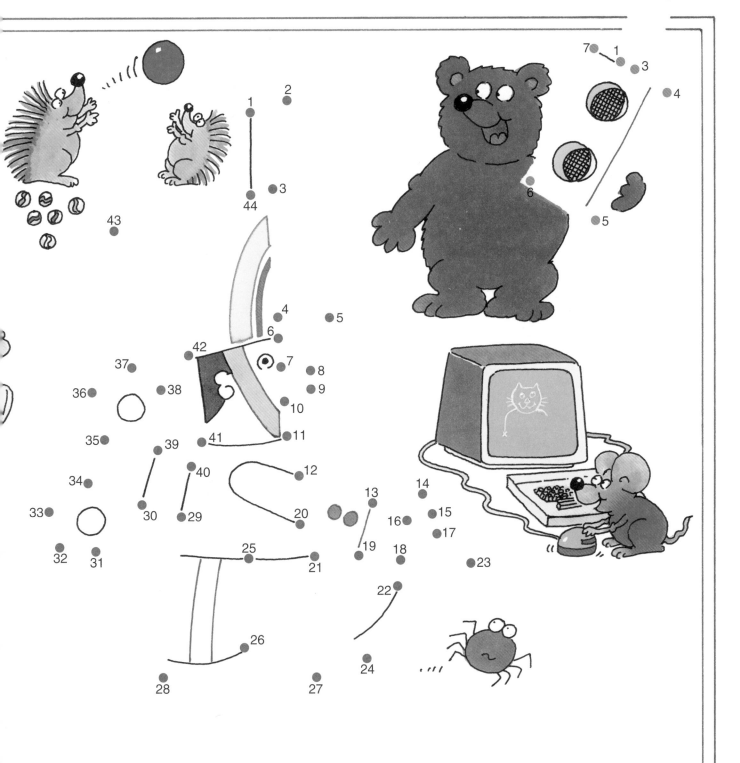

● Join the red dots. How does this toy work?

● What are pig and bear doing?

● Join the pink and blue dots to find out.

# Home machines

Mouse is busy at home.

- Join the blue dots to see what he is doing.
- Vacuum cleaners need electricity to make them work. Join the green and red dots to find more electrical machines.

# DOT-TO-DOT
# IN SPACE

# Spacesuits

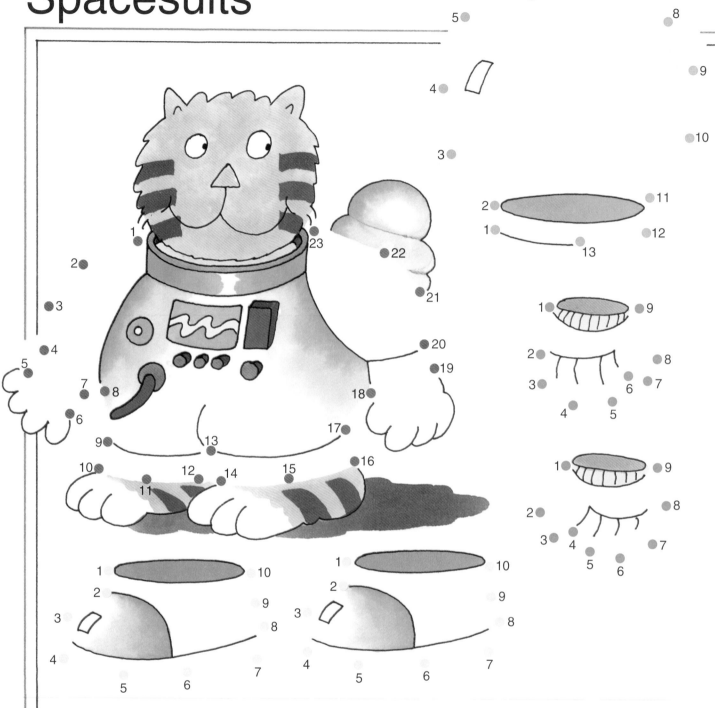

Can and mouse are trying on their spacesuits.

Join the orange dots to see the body section of cat's suit.

- Join the blue dots to find his helmet.

- If you join the green dots and the yellow dots, you will see cat's boots and gloves.

1 2 3 4 5 6 7 8 9 10 11 12 13 14 15 16 17 18 19 20 21 22 23 24 25

- Mouse is wearing his full suit. Join the purple dots to see what he looks like.

- Join the red dots to see mouse's backpack. It contains his air tanks and radio.

# Ready for blast-off

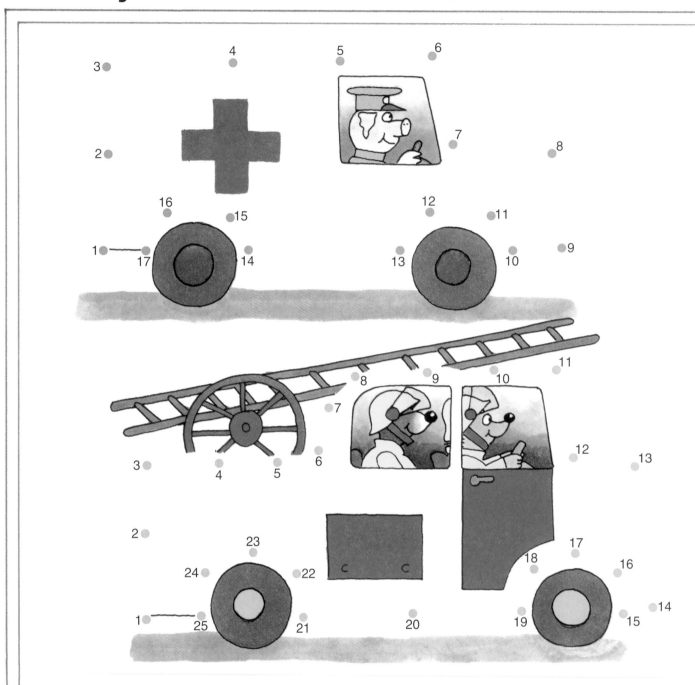

Cat and mouse are getting ready to blast off in their rocket.

- Join the red dots to see what the rocket looks like.

- If you join the yellow dots you will see the launch pad.

- There are two emergency vehicles waiting nearby. Join the green and blue dots to see what they are.

1 2 3 4 5 6 7 8 9 10 11 12 13 14 15 16 17 18 19 20 21 22 23 24 25

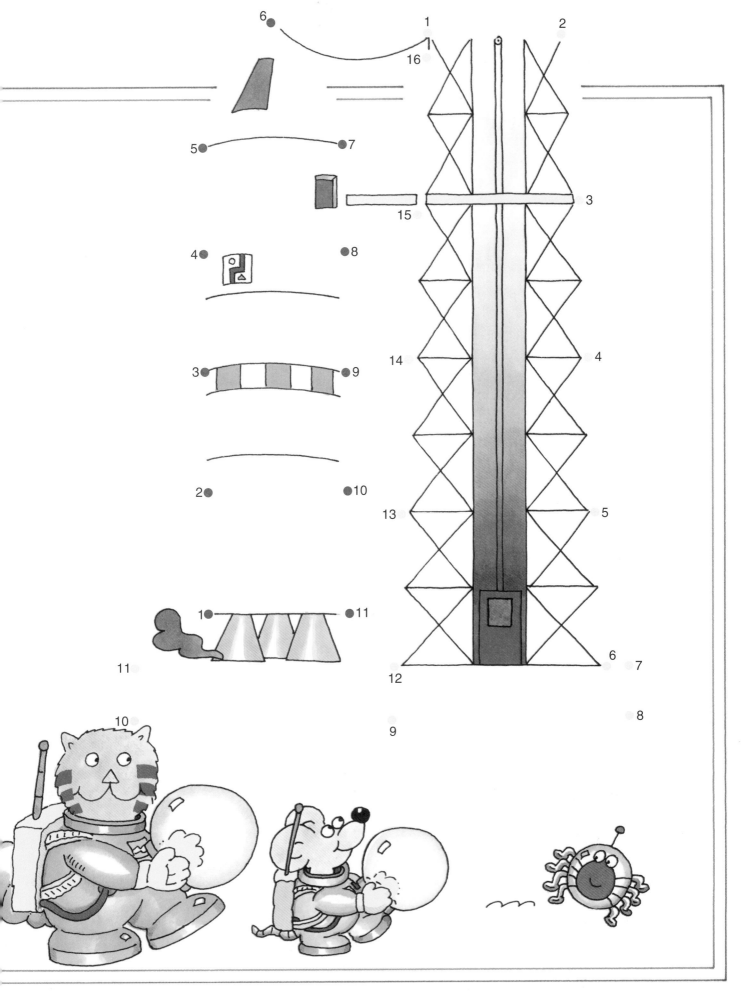

# The rocket

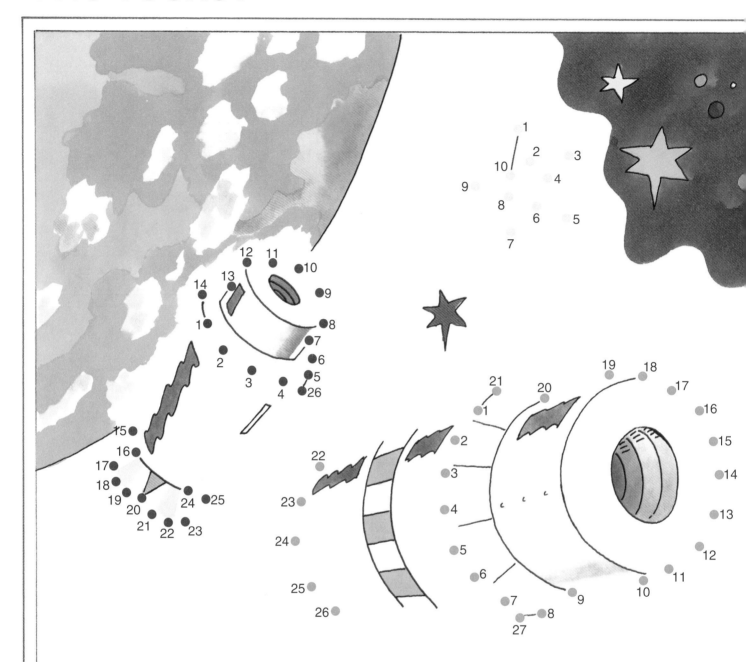

Cats and mouse's rocket is in three parts.

- Join the red dots to see the first stage of the rocket. It held the fuel needed to launch the rocket. Now the fuel has been used, it has fallen off.

- Join the green dots to see the second stage of the rocket. This took cat and mouse into orbit around the earth. Then it fell off.

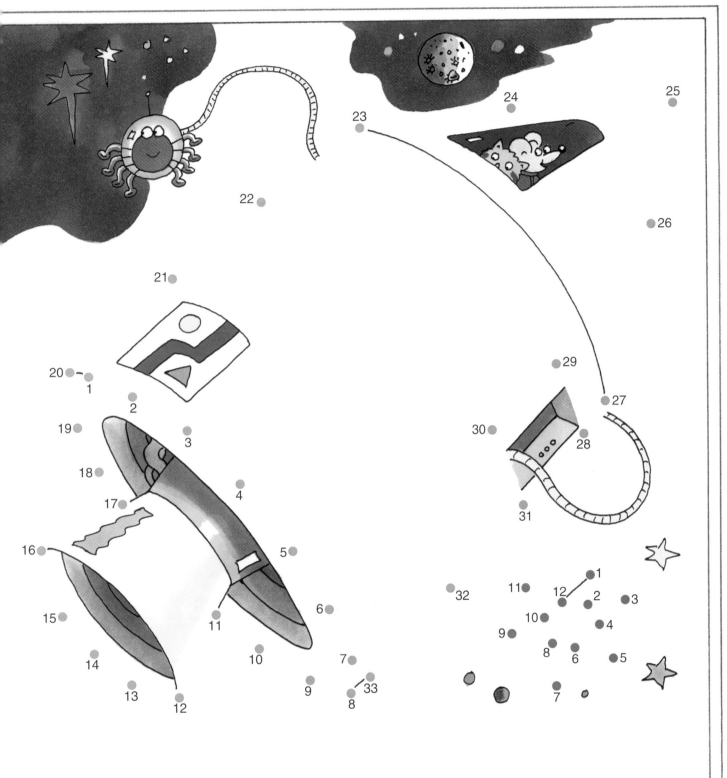

- Join the blue dots to see the part of the rocket where cat and mouse are. It is called the command module.

- What can you see if you join the yellow and orange dots?

# Inside the spacecraft

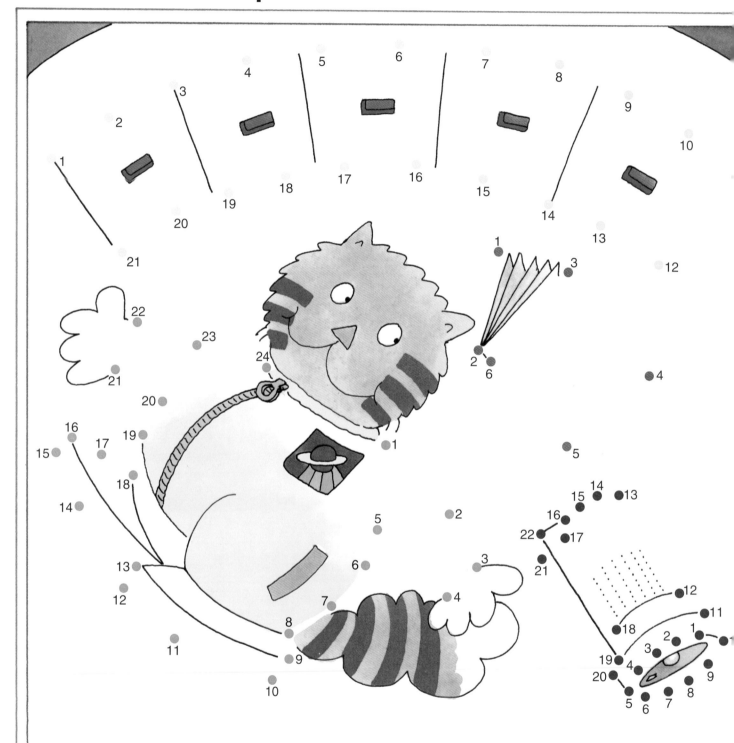

Everything is weightless inside the spacecraft. Things float around if they are not fastened in place properly.

- Join the green and blue dots to see what is happening to cat and mouse.

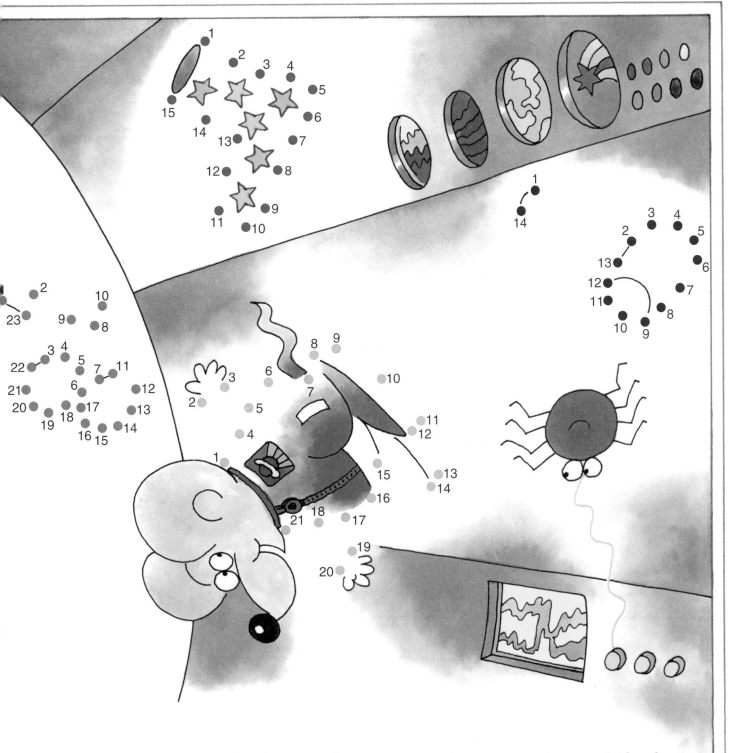

- There are special places for cat and mouse to put their equipment. Join the yellow dots to help them find them.

- If you join the rest of the dots, you will find some things that cat and mouse forgot to put away.

# A visit to a space station

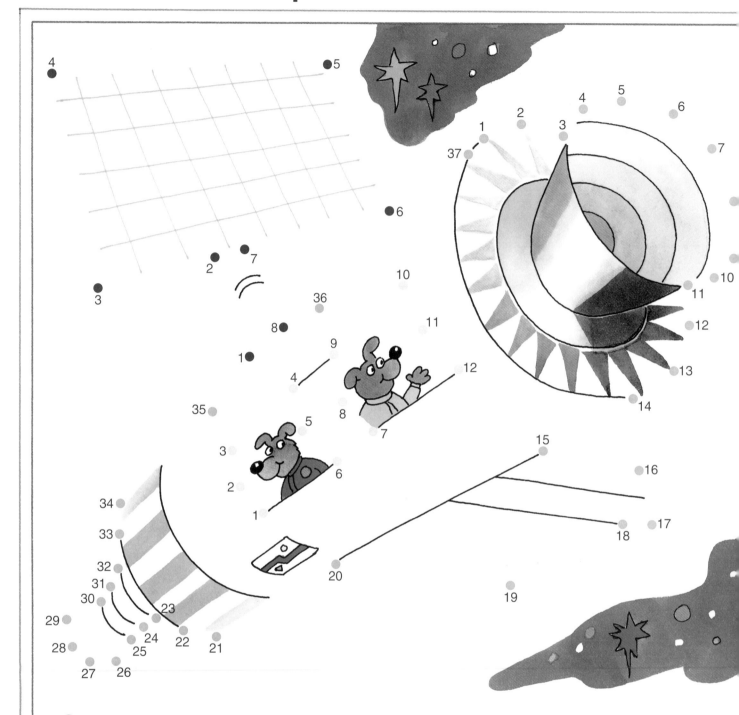

Cat and mouse's spacecraft is about to dock with
a space station.

- Join the blue dots to see what it looks like.

- Join the yellow dots to help the dogs see their visitors.

- Join the green dots to see the Earth in the distance.

1 2 3 4 5 6 7 8 9 10 11 12 13 14 15 16 17 18 19 20 21 22 23 24 25

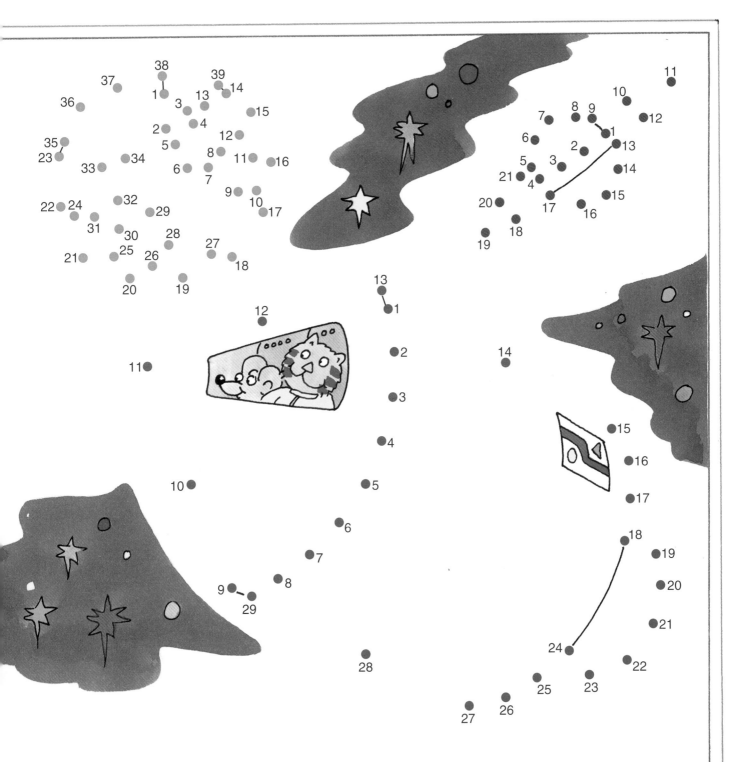

- On top of the space station is a solar panel. This provides power for all the instruments inside. Join the purple dots to see it.

- Finish the picture by joining the red and brown dots.

# Asteroids and comets

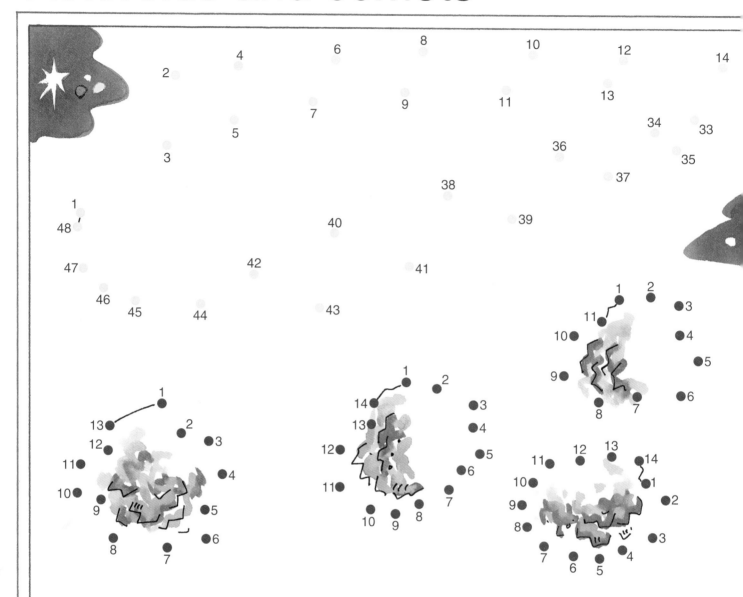

- The spacecraft has been damaged by some asteroids. Join the green dots to see what has happened.

- Asteroids are huge lumps of rock floating in space. Join the brown dots to see some of them.

- Cat is going to repair the damage. Join the blue dots to see how he is attached to the spacecraft.

- Which of cat's tools is floating away? Join the red dots.

- If you join the yellow dots, you will see a comet.

1 2 3 4 5 6 7 8 9 10 11 12 13 14 15 16 17 18 19 20 21 22 23 24 25

# On the moon

Cat and mouse have landed on the moon.

- Join the red dots to see their landing craft.
- Mouse is driving a moon buggy. Join the yellow dots to see it.

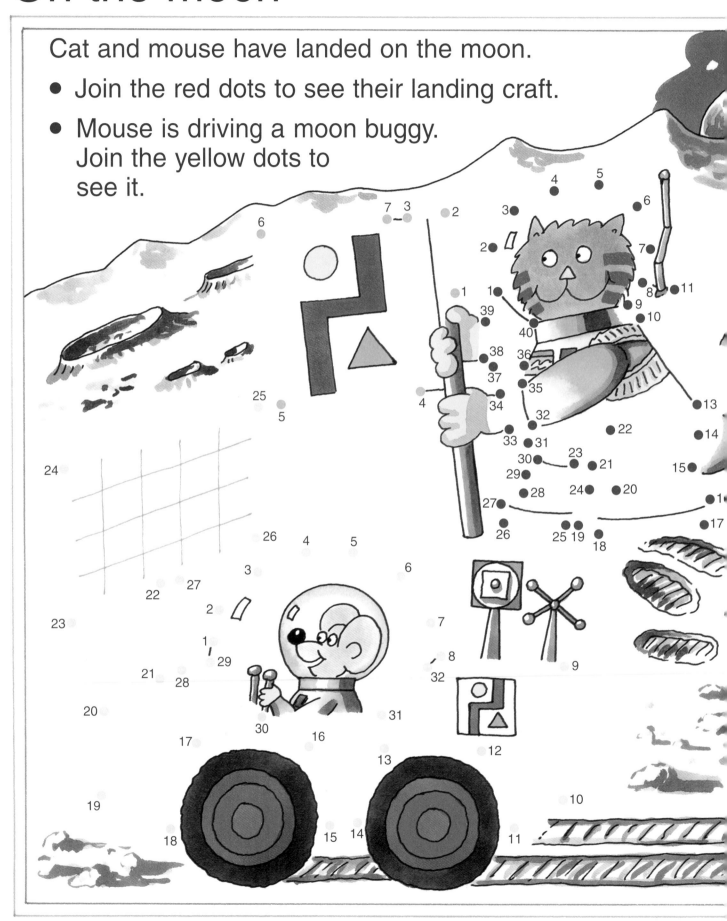

- Join the green dots to see one of the moon's craters.

- Join the blue and purple dots to see cat. What is he doing?

26 27 28 29 30 31 32 33 34 35 36 37 38 39 40 41 42 43 44 45 46 47 48 49 50

# Other spacecraft

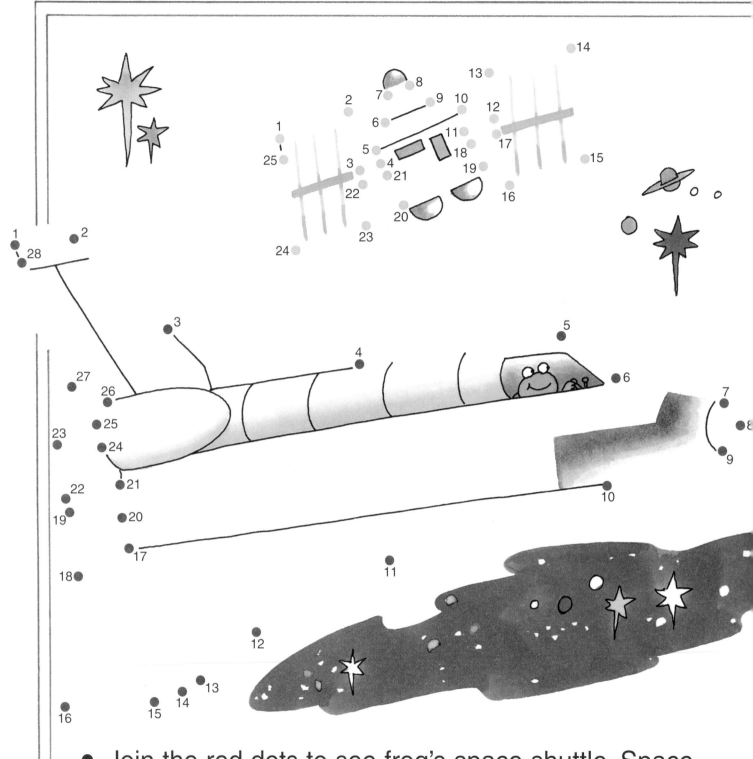

- Join the red dots to see frog's space shuttle. Space shuttles can make lots of space journeys.

- If you join the green dots you will see a satellite. Satellites are unmanned spacecraft.

1 2 3 4 5 6 7 8 9 10 11 12 13 14 15 16 17 18 19 20 21 22 23 24 25

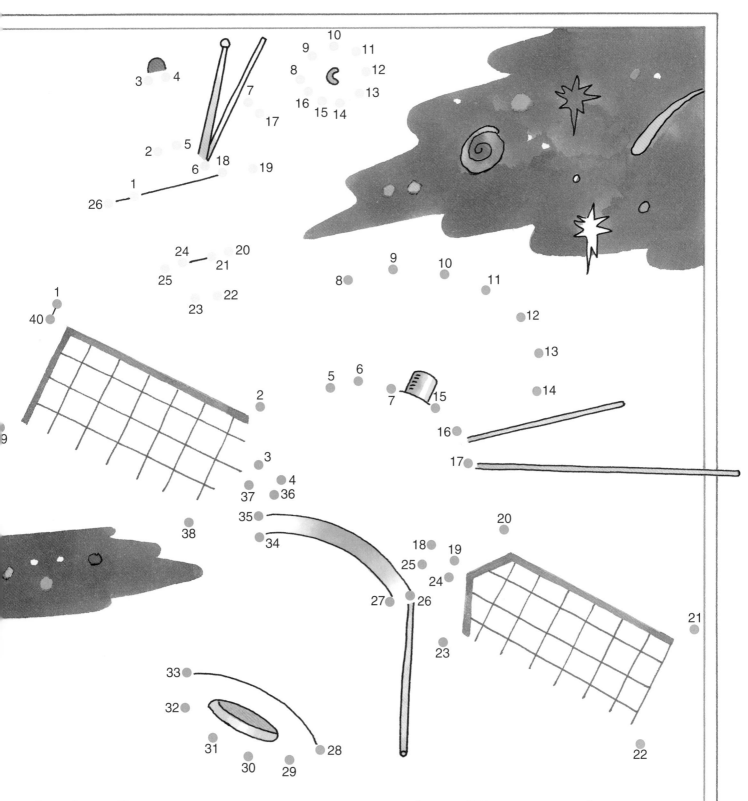

- In the distance are two space probes. These explore faraway planets and send pictures and information back to earth. Join the blue and yellow dots to see them.

# Other planets

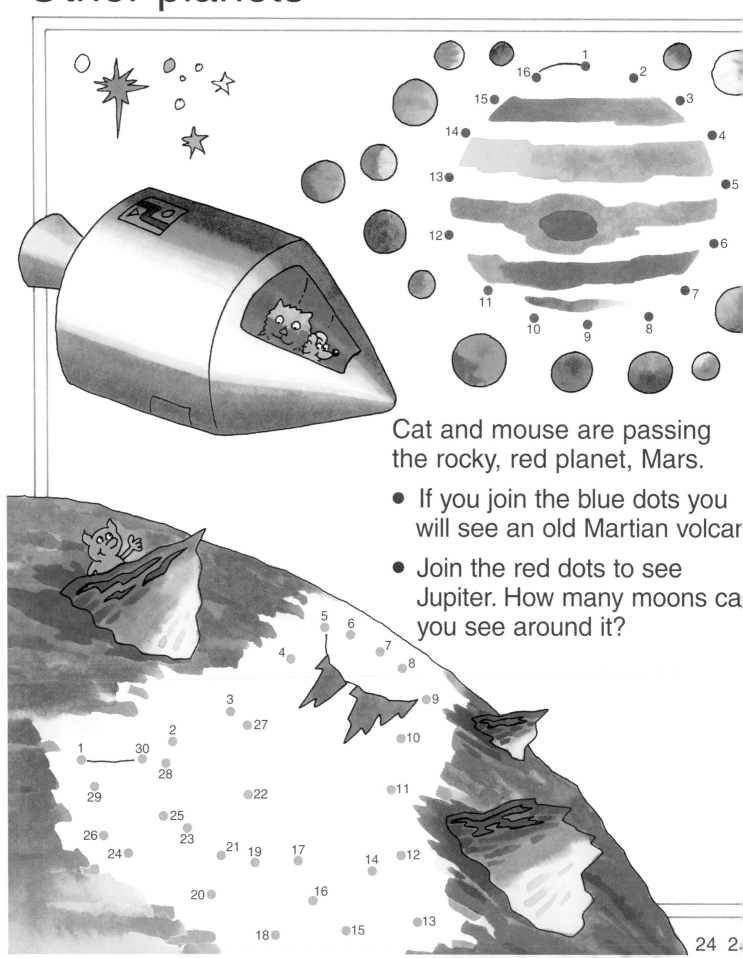

Cat and mouse are passing the rocky, red planet, Mars.

- If you join the blue dots you will see an old Martian volcar

- Join the red dots to see Jupiter. How many moons ca you see around it?

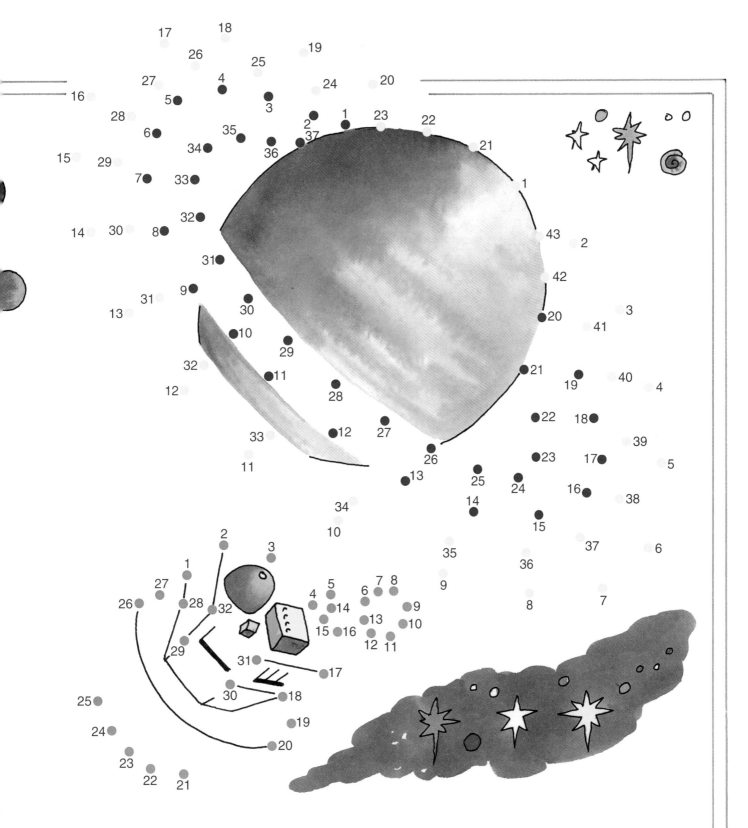

- The planet Saturn has rings around it. You can see them if you join the yellow and purple dots.

- Join the green dots to see a space probe that is investigating Saturn's rings.

26 27 28 29 30 31 32 33 34 35 36 37 38 39 40 41 42 43 44 45 46 47 48 49 50

# Space city

2

4

7  3

6

5  10

1

14

9  11

8

12

13

15

4

2

3

11

10

13

1

8

9  12

6

5

7

Cat and mouse think they must be dreaming. They seem to have found an alien space city.

- Join the red dots to see what it looks like.
- Join the the yellow, green and blue dots to see the aliens' spacecraft.

1 2 3 4 5 6 7 8 9 10 11 12 13 14 15 16 17 18 19 20 21 22 23 24 25

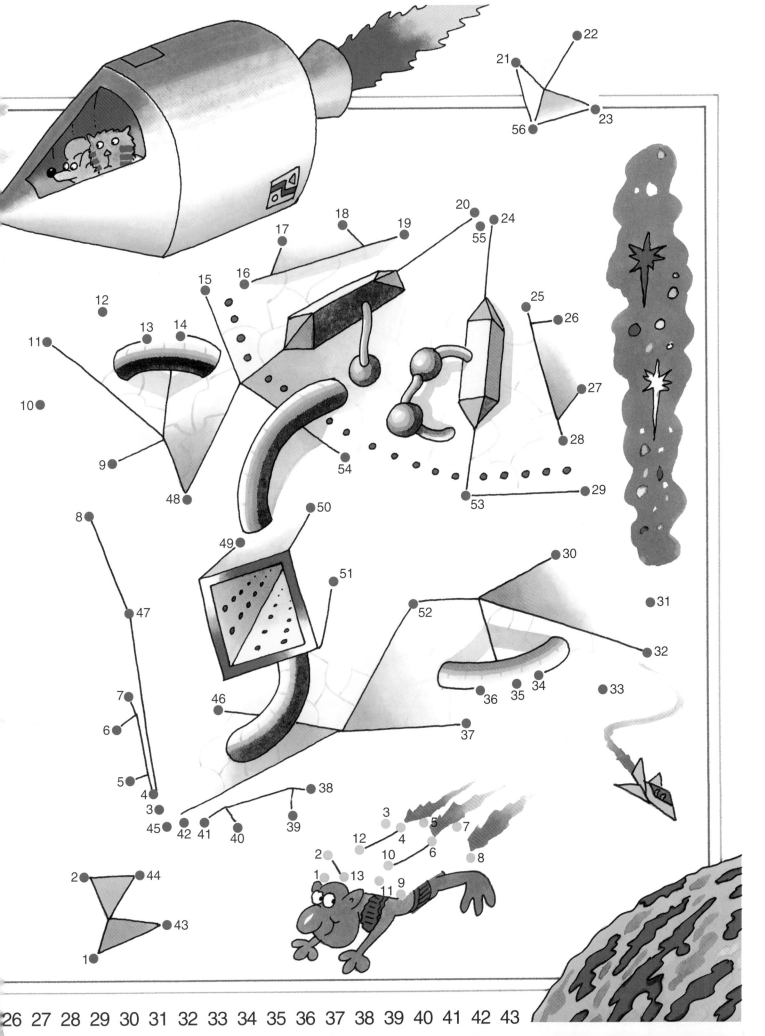

# Splashdown

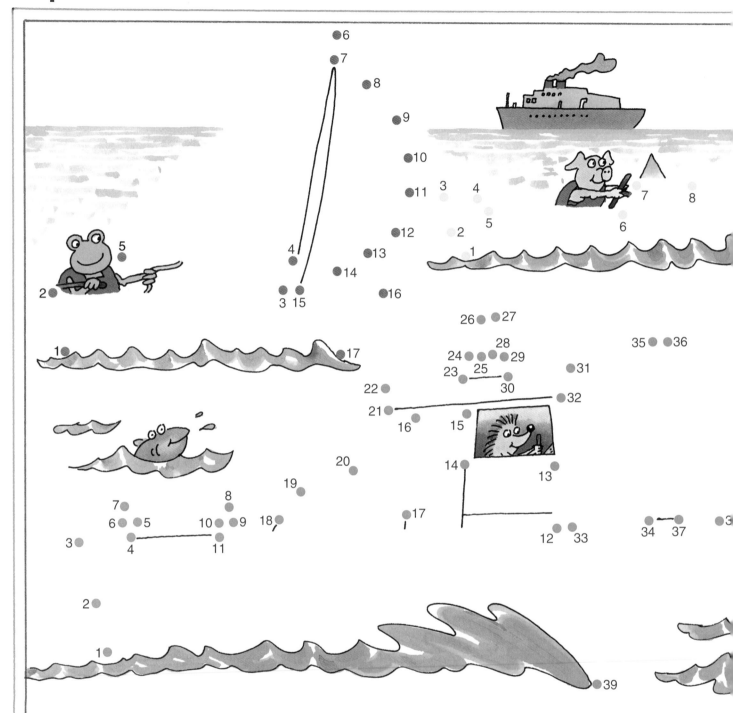

Cat and mouse are returning to earth.

- The command module is about to splash down into the ocean. Join the red dots to see it.

- Join the blue dots to see what slowed it down as it feel to earth.

1 2 3 4 5 6 7 8 9 10 11 12 13 14 15 16 17 18 19 20 21 22 23 24 25

● There is a rescue boat waiting to pick up cat and mouse. Join the green dots to see it.

● Frog and pig have come to help. Join the pink and yellow dots to see how they got there.

# Home again

Cat and mouse are back home. They are looking into space to see where they have been.

- Join the green and blue dots to see the special equipment they are using.

- Join the red dots to see somewhere that cat and mouse visited.

# DOT-TO-DOT
# NATURE

# In the Arctic

Cat and mouse are going on a World Nature Tour.
They have just landed on the ice pack near the North Pole.

- Join the green dots to see how they got there.

- What has cat spotted? Join the blue dots to see.

1 2 3 4 5 6 7 8 9 10 11 12 13 14 15 16 17 18 19 20 21 22 23 24 25

- What do you see if you join the yellow dots?
- Mouse is taking a photograph of a walrus.
  Join the red dots to see it. Notice its two long tusks.

26 27 28 29 30 31 32 33 34 35 36 37 38 39 40 41 42 43 44 45 46 47 48 49 50

# In the tundra

Cat and mouse travel south to land called the tundra.
In winter it is very snowy.

- Help cat and mouse find out what flowers they have found.
  Join the orange dots to see some Arctic poppies.
  Join the yellow dots to see some purple saxifrage.

1 2 3 4 5 6 7 8 9 10 11 12 13 14 15 16 17 18 19 20 21 22 23 24 25

- Join the red dots to see a shaggy-coated musk ox.
- If you join the blue dots, you will see a caribou.
- Join the green dots to find an animal that hunts these two animals.

# Up a mountain

Cat and mouse are climbing a high mountain to see the plants and animals that live there.

● What can they see if you join the green dots?

1 2 3 4 5 6 7 8 9 10 11 12 13 14 15 16 17 18 19 20 21 22 23 24 25

- If you join the red dots, you will find an ibex.
- Join the blue dots. This animal is called an alpine marmot.

26 27 28 29 30 31 32 33 34 35 36 37 38 39 40 41 42 43 44 45 46 47 48 49 50

# In a field

Cat and mouse's helicopter has landed in a field.

- Who is cat watching? Join the blue dots to see.
- Join the yellow dots to see who is watching mouse.

1 2 3 4 5 6 7 8 9 10 11 12 13 14 15 16 17 18 19 20 21 22 23 24 25

- Join the green dots to see what mouse is drawing.
- Join the red dots to see an ox-eye daisy.

26 27 28 29 30 31 32 33 34 35 36 37 38 39 40 41 42 43 44 45 46 47 48 49 50

# In the forest

Join the red dots. What kind of tree can you see?

What can you see if you join the blue dots?

1 2 3 4 5 6 7 8 9 10 11 12 13 14 15 16 17 18 19 20 21 22 23 24 25

- Cat has climbed a tree to get a better view of a red crossbill. Join the yellow dots so you can see it too.

- Do you know what a chipmunk looks like? Find out by joining the green dots.

# In the desert

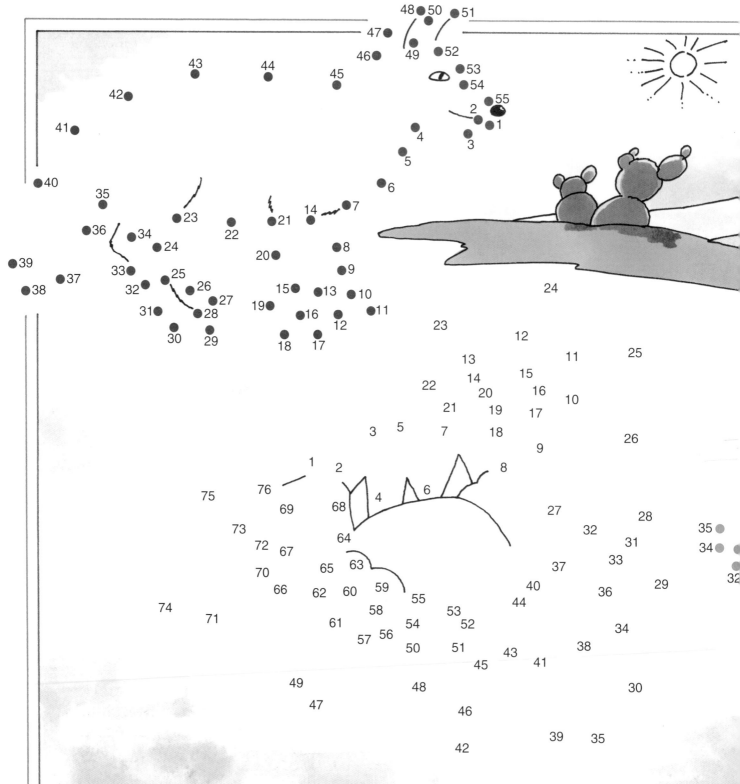

Cat and mouse have landed in the desert.

- Join the blue dots to see a plant that stores water in its stem.

1 2 3 4 5 6 7 8 9 10 11 12 13 14 15 16 17 18 19 20 21 22 23 24 25

- Join the red dots to see an animal called a coyote.
- If you join the yellow dots, you will see a scorpion.
- Join the green dots to see a road runner.

# In the rainforest

- What is cat watching through his binoculars?
  Join the red dots to see.

- Join the green dots to see what is growing on the tree.

1 2 3 4 5 6 7 8 9 10 11 12 13 14 15 16 17 18 19 20 21 22 23 24 25

- Join the yellow dots to see one of the creatures that flies in the forest.
- Join the blue dots to see who is interested in mouse.

# Grasslands

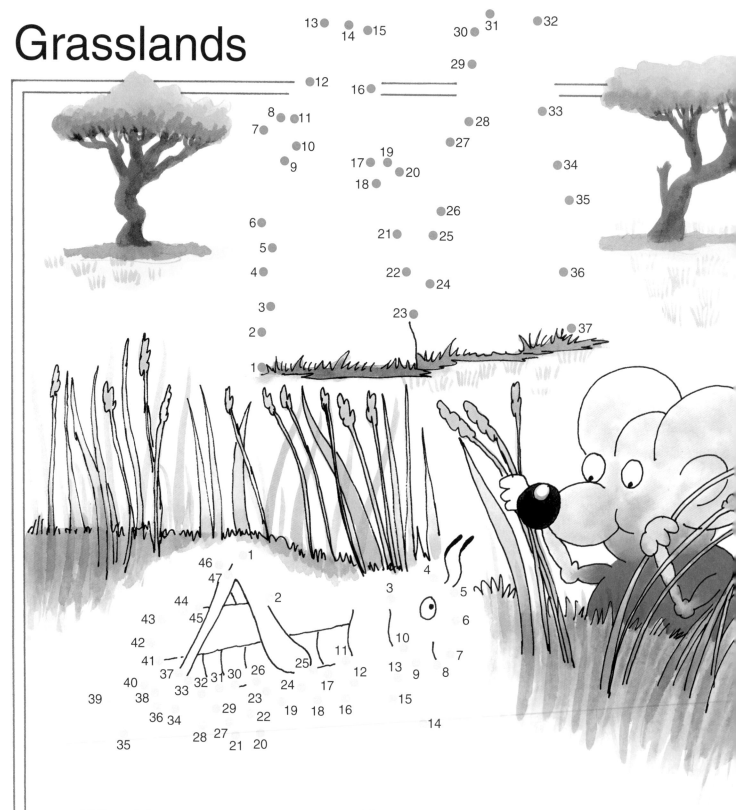

- What has mouse spotted? You can see it too by joining the yellow dots.

- Join the green dots. These hills were made by insects called termites.

1 2 3 4 5 6 7 8 9 10 11 12 13 14 15 16 17 18 19 20 21 22 23 24 25

- The baobab tree stores a lot of water in its huge trunk. Help cat find out how big it is by joining the blue dots.

- What do you see when you join the red dots?

# A coral reef

Cat and mouse are swimming around the coral in the warm sea.

● What can you see if you join the red dots?

1 2 3 4 5 6 7 8 9 10 11 12 13 14 15 16 17 18 19 20 21 22 23 24 25

- What creatures are swimming with cat and mouse? Join the blue and yellow dots to see.

- Finish the coral reef by joining the green and purple dots.

# Australia

Cat and mouse have discovered some animals that live only in Australia.

● There are lots of eucalyptus trees in Australia. Join the blue dots to find an animal which eats their leaves.

1 2 3 4 5 6 7 8 9 10 11 12 13 14 15 16 17 18 19 20 21 22 23 24 25

8
9
7
10
4 5 6 11
2 3 12
13
14
15
16
21 22 25
17 24 26
23 27
18 20 28
19 29
30

1
62
61 60
59 58
57 56

5
4
3 6 7 31
2 8 32 33 37
54 34 36 38
55 36 39 40
53 35 41
46 52 51 50 49 48 47 43 42 44
47 45 45 46

10
11
44 12
43 36
37 13
40 35
42 38
41 39 34 14
33 15
32 16
22 17 18
30 31 20 19
29 27 23 21
28 26 25 24

- Mouse is birdwatching. He has spotted a kookaburra and a parrot. Join the red and green dots to see them too.

- What can you see when you join the yellow dots?

# The Antarctic

Cat and mouse are on the last stop of their tour.
They are now near the South Pole.

- Join the green dots to see an albatross. Each of its wings
  is as long as a person.

1 2 3 4 5 6 7 8 9 10 11 12 13 14 15 16 17 18 19 20 21 22 23 24 25

Seven types of penguin live in the Antarctic.

- Join the blue dots to see the smallest. It is called a rockhopper.
- Join the yellow dots to see the largest. This is an emperor penguin.
- Mouse is sketching an elephant seal. Join the red dots to see it.

26 27 28 29 30 31 32 33 34 35 36 37 38 39 40 41 42 43 44 45 46 47 48 49 50

# Back home

Cat and mouse are looking through the photographs
they took on their trip.

- Join the red and blue dots to see the ones they like best.

- Look back through the book and see if you can find out
  where these photographs were taken.